Jonathan Swift

THE PROFILES IN LITERATURE SERIES

GENERAL EDITOR: B. C. SOUTHAM, M.A., B.LITT. (OXON.)
*Formerly Department of English, Westfield College,
University of London*

Volumes in the series include

CHARLOTTE BRONTË	Arthur Pollard *University of Hull*
CHARLES DICKENS	Martin Fido, *University of Leeds*
HENRY FIELDING	C. J. Rawson, *University of Warwick*
JAMES JOYCE	Arnold Goldman, *University of Sussex*
HERMAN MELVILLE	D. E. S. Maxwell, *Professor of English, York Univ. Toronto*
THOMAS LOVE PEACOCK	Carl Dawson, *University of California*
SAMUEL RICHARDSON	A. M. Kearney, *Chorley College of Education*
WALTER SCOTT	Robin Mayhead, *University of Ghana*
ZOLA	Philip Walker, *University of California*

Jonathan Swift

by *Kathleen Williams*
Professor of English Literature
University of California

LONDON
ROUTLEDGE & KEGAN PAUL
NEW YORK: HUMANITIES PRESS

10627

First published 1968
by Routledge and Kegan Paul Ltd
Broadway House, 68–74 Carter Lane
London, E.C.4

© Kathleen Williams 1968

Printed in Great Britain
by Northumberland Press Limited
Gateshead

SBN 7100 2948 9

The Profiles in Literature Series

This series is designed to provide the student of literature and the general reader with a brief and helpful introduction to the major novelists and prose writers in English, American and foreign literature.

Each volume will provide an account of an individual author's writing career and works, through a series of carefully chosen extracts illustrating the major aspects of the author's art. These extracts are accompanied by commentary and analysis, drawing attention to particular features of the style and treatment. There is no pretence, of course, that a study of extracts can give a sense of the works as a whole, but this selective approach enables the reader to focus his attention upon specific features, and to be informed in his approach by experienced critics and scholars who are contributing to the series.

The volumes will provide a particularly helpful and practical form of introduction to writers whose works are extensive or which present special problems for the modern reader, who can then proceed with a sense of his bearings and an informed eye for the writer's art.

An important feature of these books is the extensive reference list of the author's works and the descriptive list of the most useful biographies, commentaries and critical studies.

B.C.S.

Contents

Jonathan Swift—his life and works

Jonathan Swift (1667–1745) was born, of English parents, in Ireland, where he was to spend the greater part of his life. He was educated at Trinity College, Dublin, but much of his considerable learning was attained in the library of Moor Park, in Surrey, where he lived for some years as secretary and general helper to Sir William Temple, a cultivated retired statesman with literary interests. He took holy orders in 1695, and on Temple's death in 1699 went to take up permanent residence in his parish in Ireland. In the 1690s he had already written two important works (not published until 1704), *The Battle of the Books*, a gay contribution to that discussion of the merits of modern, as compared to ancient and classical authors, which engaged so many in seventeenth-century England and France, and the brilliant *A Tale of a Tub*, which is, in his own accurate description, an exposure of 'the Abuses and Corruptions in Learning and Religion'.

In an age when good writing could bring advancement in church or state, the evidence of 'wit', or intellectual power, and of learning in the *Tale* earned Swift the notice first of his superiors in the Irish Church, who sent him to

England to conduct an important mission to the Whig government, and then of the English Tory opposition, who enlisted his help to write in their cause. This he was the more ready to do because the Tories regarded themselves as supporters of the established church, and during the Tory administration of 1710 to the death of Queen Anne in 1714 he had great influence though no official standing. Through his political satires and tracts he helped to bring about results which were close to his heart. But when the government fell he returned to Ireland, now as Dean of St. Patrick's Cathedral in Dublin, and the second period of his political power was in the 1720s, when he upheld the rights of the Irish parliament and people against the Whig administration of Walpole in England. With *The Drapier's Letters* he again achieved at least a temporary success, and his courage made him the idol of the people, 'the Drapier', 'the Irish patriot', 'the great Dean'. In this period of successful practical activity, also, he wrote *Gulliver's Travels* (published in 1726) and as Dean he did much for the physical as well as the moral welfare of his people.

But Swift's efforts to fight oppression, and to arouse the oppressed themselves to fight it, had no permanent results; and his disappointment, and his increasing loneliness as his old friends died, made his last years sorrowful and even bitter. In his old age he outlived his bodily and mental health. But in that last state he neither wrote nor spoke. His great satires were finished long before, when his mind was at its clearest and most brilliant, and his capacity for savage indignation, amusement, and pity at its strongest. Swift was too sane to be complacent, and this is one reason why he is so great a satirist.

But Swift owes his commanding position as the most powerful and also the most subtle of English prose satirists not only to qualities which we usually regard as personal ones—passion, humour, honesty, courage, intelligence, moral conviction—but to qualities which are more obviously literary, such as imagination, inventiveness, and stylistic and rhetorical skill. Like all his educated contemporaries he was trained in the art of rhetoric—that is, in the art of so handling one's words, sentences, figures of speech, arguments, that the audience or reader is persuaded to accept a particular point of view. And Swift had gifts which enabled him to make the most of this training. He had, for example, an excellent ear for all kinds of talk and tones of voice. He can capture the turn of speech of a ship's doctor, a footman, a fashionable lady, a pedantic scholar. But more than this, his sensitivity to nuances of speech is also a sensitivity to nuances of meaning and of character. Especially he is able to simulate the tone of the deceiving and of the self-deceived : of an economist who can imagine no relation between the governing and the governed but that of exploitation, of a writer on Christianity who has no conception of what religion is. In fact he can capture the rhetoric by which men seek to persuade others, and themselves, for their own ends, and in capturing it he exposes it for what it is, and shows the moral confusion and emptiness that lie beneath the persuasive words.

This is a skill which involves at once moral perception, imagination, and magnificent verbal control. And unless we appreciate the detailed precision of that verbal control, the moral and imaginative power will not be fully recognised. A great satirist is a man with intense convictions about right and wrong, but his convictions must be made to convince us too; and for this he needs a sharp insight into the delusions and the wishful thinking which complicate our actual daily lives, and a capacity to make these things vivid to us in words. Swift's typical strategy is to adopt a way of writing which reveals a way of thinking. The parody of a literary style becomes a parody of a mental style. In the terms of his modern critics, Swift employs a series of 'mouthpieces', 'personae', or 'masks', and makes them betray themselves as they write or speak. So where lesser satirists tell us that it is foolish and wrong to be an opportunist, or to exploit others, or to deceive oneself, Swift shows us these errors revealing themselves in the words of the 'authors' of *A Tale of a Tub*, *A Modest Proposal*, or *Gulliver's Travels*. We do not merely agree with the moral evaluations implied; we have lived, in our imaginations, through a moral experience. Swift's power to shock us into fresh insights—whereas so much satire is dully predictable—lies in such skills as these.

It is for this reason that the extracts in this volume direct attention to such verbal and stylistic matters as parody, irony, use of metaphor, choice of words. We must be able to recognise the precise tone in which (for instance) Gulliver is made to comment on the moral position of the King of Brobdingnag or of the master Houyhnhnm, before we are able to follow out the complex web of ironies which define Swift's meanings. Only through awareness of his use of words can we recognise what it is that he is telling us (and telling us with intellectual precision as well as with emotional and moral force) about the pitfalls that we prepare for ourselves, and duly fall into, in our daily lives. Swift has very exact things to convey to us, and things that are still valuable, stimulating, and true; for although he writes in terms of the ideas and events of his own day he recognises in these the enduring habits of men. He speaks an old language, but he speaks to us. But the old language must be understood; and so some of the extracts which follow point to the contemporary and everyday matters by means of which Swift comments upon unchanging humanity.

In considering Swift's writings we must remember above all that he is, first and last, a satirist and also, so he himself would rightly have claimed, a moralist, whose aim is to reveal us to ourselves, to make us see ourselves afresh and from a new angle, so that we suddenly recognise the triviality, the irrationality, the hypocrisy and the careless cruelty of so much that we think and do. Daily habit or the clichés of literary, political, or even moral theorising can readily blind us to our own and our society's foolishness or evil, and the satirist must surprise and shock us into clarity of vision.

To this end, all Swift's literary skills are turned, and only in relation to this end can they be appreciated and understood. He can imitate a particular style, that of the scientist or of the Hermetic philosopher, but his purpose is to show by this means the self-indulgence which so often confuses our thinking. He can tell a fine adventure story, but his purpose is to show our capacity to go through new experiences with closed minds, learning from them only what we wish to learn. He can create new creatures and a succession of new countries, he can write with the metaphoric complexity of a poet. And usually he is employing several such methods at once, for Swift's art is essentially one of complication, indirection, and surprise, and we must be ready to respond to many effects simultaneously. To take at their face value the stories that Gulliver, or the nameless 'author' of *A Tale of a Tub*, have to tell us would be wholly to miss the brilliance of their creator's comic and satiric art, and the acuteness of his insight into the nature of men. Swift is a satirist who compels us, by the complexity and indirection of his ironic methods, to be alert and aware at every point. In the end, his greatness is his power to make us think, and feel, for ourselves.

Scheme of extracts

The extracts which follow are all instances of Swift's subtly varied satiric methods. All involve irony: that is, they are not straightforward statements of Swift's own point of view, but they imply it in indirect ways. Swift's intention is not, primarily, to *tell* us what he believes to be wrong or mistaken in our attitudes or actions, but to make us work this out for ourselves in reading. His ironic indirection achieves this end.

Each extract is written as though by someone other than Jonathan Swift himself; that is, he uses a persona, or mouthpiece, through whom he can work indirectly. Sometimes the persona is named, as a distinct person (Gulliver, the Drapier), sometimes he is unnamed and less definite. In such cases we recognise the kind of person he is through his style and opinions. Sometimes the persona's opinions are very like Swift's own, but sometimes the persona's manner and views show him to be a foolish, or a self-interested, or a morally obtuse person, whose views cannot be accepted, but are only an indirect way of showing such views as they really are, and of implying more adequate ones.

6

Satiric use of apparently straightforward narrative

In this extract, what appears to be an innocent and straight-forwardly presented story turns out to be a satiric allegorical narrative about the history of the Christian Churches up to Swift's time. The chief characters are three brothers, Peter (the Roman Catholic Church); Martin, named for Luther (the Anglican Church); and Jack, named for Calvin (the Nonconformist or dissenting churches). Swift adopts a simple style for his persona, the story-teller, who here professes merely to record accurately an old, true history, without drawing conclusions from it or seeing it as having allegorical meaning. But the actions of the brothers are an allegory of the errors of the churches. The will (the Gospel) left by the heroes' father has instructed them not to decorate the plain coats they originally wore, but over the years, under the guidance of Peter from whom the other brothers had not yet separated at the Reformation, they have over-laid their coats with ornaments of lace and embroidery (ceremonies and dogmas are added to the simple worship of the early church), and have become worldly. When he realises how far this process has gone, and how much his coat has changed, Jack angrily tears off the decorations to return to his father's will. But in doing so he tears the fabric of the coat itself (damages, by too thorough a reformation, necessary religious practices and beliefs). Martin also reforms, but in the moderate Anglican way, discarding only such traditions as may be abandoned without harm to important aspects of Christianity. The story implies, however, that even Martin is faulty compared with the commands of the Gospel and the will of God for the churches.

I

I record, therefore, that brother Jack, brimful of this miraculous compound, reflecting with indignation upon Peter's tyranny, and farther provoked by the despondency of Martin, prefaced his resolutions to this purpose. 'What,' said he, 'a rogue that locked up his drink, turned away our wives, cheated us of our fortunes, palmed his damned crusts upon us for mutton, and at last kicked us out of doors; must we be in his fashions, with a pox? A rascal, besides, that all the street cries out against.' Having thus kindled and inflamed himself as high as possible, and by consequence, in a delicate temper for beginning a reformation, he set about the work immediately, and in three minutes made more dispatch than Martin had done in as many hours. For (courteous reader) you are given to understand, that zeal is never so highly obliged, as when you set it a-tearing; and Jack, who doated on that quality in himself, allowed it at this time its full swing. Thus it happened, that stripping down a parcel of gold lace a little too hastily, he rent the main body of his coat from top to bottom; and whereas his talent was not of the happiest in taking up a stitch, he knew no better way than to darn it again with packthread and a skewer. But the matter was yet infinitely worse (I record it with tears) when he proceeded to the embroidery: for, being clumsy by nature,

8

and of temper impatient; withal, beholding millions of stitches that required the nicest hand, and sedatest constitutions, to extricate; in a great rage he tore off the whole piece, cloth and all, and flung it into the kennel, and furiously thus continuing his career: 'Ah, good brother Martin,' said he, 'do as I do, for the love of God; strip, tear, pull, rend, flay off all, that we may appear as unlike the rogue Peter as it is possible. I would not for a hundred pounds carry the least mark about me, that might give occasion to the neighbours of suspecting I was related to such a rascal.' But Martin, who at this time happened to be extremely phlegmatic and sedate, begged his brother, of all love, not to damage his coat by any means; for he never would get such another : desired him to consider, that it was not their business to form their actions by any reflection upon Peter, but by observing the rules prescribed in their father's will. That he should remember, Peter was still their brother, whatever faults or injuries he had committed; and therefore they should by all means avoid such a thought as that of taking measures for good and evil, from no other rule than of opposition to him. That it was true, the testament of their good father was very exact in what related to the wearing of their coats; yet was it no less penal and strict in prescribing agreement, and friendship, and affection between them. And therefore, if straining a point were at all dispensible, it would certainly be so rather to the advance of unity than increase of contradiction.

Martin had still proceeded as gravely as he began, and doubtless would have delivered an admirable lecture of morality, which might have exceedingly contributed to my reader's repose, both of body and mind (the true ultimate end of ethics); but Jack was already gone a flightshot beyond his patience. And as in scholastic disputes, nothing serves to rouse the spleen of him that opposes, so much as a kind of pedantic affected calmness in the respondent; disputants being for the most part like unequal scales, where the gravity of one side advances the lightness of the other, and causes it to fly up and kick the beam; so it happened here that the weight of Martin's argument exalted Jack's levity, and made him fly out and spurn against his brother's moderation. In short, Martin's patience put Jack in a rage; but that which most afflicted him was, to observe his brother's coat so well reduced into the state of innocence; while his own was either wholly rent to his shirt, or those places which had escaped his cruel clutches, were still in Peter's livery. So that he looked like a drunken beau, half rifled by bullies; or like a fresh tenant of Newgate, when he has refused the payment of garnish; or like a discovered shoplifter left to the mercy of Exchange women; or like a bawd in her old velvet petticoat, resigned into the secular hands of the mobile. Like any or like all of these, a medley of rags, and lace, and rents, and fringes, unfortunately Jack did now appear: he would have been extremely glad to see his coat in the condition of Martin's, but infinitely gladder to find that of Martin's in the same predicament with his. However, since neither of these was likely to come to pass, he thought fit to lend the whole business another turn, and to dress up necessity into a virtue. Therefore, after as many of the fox's arguments as he could muster up, for bringing Martin to reason, as he called it; or, as he meant it, into his own ragged, bobtailed condition; and observing he said all to little purpose; what, alas, was left for the forlorn Jack to do, but after a million of scurrilities against his brother, to run mad with spleen, and spite, and contradiction. To be short, here began a mortal breach between these two. Jack went immediately to new lodgings, and in a few days it was for certain reported, that he had run out of his wits. In a short time after he appeared abroad, and confirmed the report by falling into the oddest whimseys that ever a sick brain conceived.

A Tale of a Tub, Section VI

Swift's satiric allegory owes much of its force to its neat

and appropriate details, and these should be examined. What, for example, is allegorically referred to in each item of Jack's condemnation of Peter's overbearing behaviour?

Swift gains satiric effect by the comparisons employed in describing the appearance of Jack, the excitable and emotional dissenting preacher, and by Jack's rough and uneducated manner of speech.

His method enables him to imply that all the churches have their limitations. Martin is gently mocked for his gravity and calmness (the Anglican claim to moderation, the 'middle way', must make him seem a little dull compared with his more extreme and excitable brothers).

Satiric use of apparently straightforward description

Of the four parts or books of *Gulliver's Travels* (each a voyage lived through and related by Swift's invented character Lemuel Gulliver) each one examines human behaviour from a different point of view, and the peoples and countries are invented for that purpose. In the first book, for example, Gulliver visits a nation of tiny men, in whom human moral 'smallness' and pettiness is shown. On his fourth voyage Gulliver is set ashore in a country populated not by human beings, of any size, but by horses which can reason and speak (the Houyhnhnms), whose beasts of burden, the Yahoos, are animals shaped like men and having human instincts and passions, but lacking the power of reason which human beings and Houyhnhnms possess. Gulliver here describes his first sight of the Yahoos, and his reactions to them on that occasion.

2

Upon the 9th day of May, 1711, one James Welch came down to my cabin; and said he had orders from the captain to set me ashore. I expostulated with him, but in vain;

neither would he so much as tell me who their new captain was. They forced me into the long-boat, letting me put on my best suit of clothes, which were as good as new, and a small bundle of linen, but no arms except my hanger; and they were so civil as not to search my pockets, into which I conveyed what money I had, with some other little necessaries. They rowed about a league, and then set me down on a strand. I desired them to tell me what country it was. They all swore, they knew no more than myself, but said, that the captain (as they called him) was resolved, after they had sold the lading, to get rid of me in the first place where they discovered land. They pushed off immediately, advising me to make haste, for fear of being overtaken by the tide, and bade me farewell.

In this desolate condition I advanced forward, and soon got upon firm ground, where I sat down on a bank to rest myself, and consider what I had best to do. When I was a little refreshed I went up into the country, resolving to deliver myself to the first savages I should meet, and purchase my life from them by some bracelets, glass rings, and other toys, which sailors usually provide themselves with in those voyages, and whereof I had some about me : the land was divided by long rows of trees, not regularly planted, but naturally growing; there was great plenty of grass, and several fields of oats. I walked very circumspectly for fear of being surprised, or suddenly shot with an arrow from behind or on either side. I fell into a beaten road, where I saw many tracks of human feet, and some of cows, but most of horses. At last I beheld several animals in a field, and one or two of the same kind sitting in trees. Their shape was very singular, and deformed, which a little discomposed me, so that I lay down behind a thicket to observe them better. Some of them coming forward near the place where I lay, gave me an opportunity of distinctly marking their form. Their heads and breasts were covered with a thick hair, some frizzled and others lank; they had beards like goats, and a long ridge of hair down their backs, and the foreparts of their legs and feet, but the rest of their bodies were bare, so that I might see their skins, which were of a brown buff colour. They had no tails, nor any hair at all on their buttocks, except about the anus; which, I presume, nature had placed there to defend them as they sat on the ground; for this posture they used, as well as lying down, and often stood on their hind feet. They climbed high trees, as nimbly as a squirrel, for they had strong extended claws before and behind, terminating in sharp points, and hooked. They would often spring, and bound, and leap with prodigious agility. The females were not so large as the males; they had long lank hair on their heads, and only a sort of down on the rest of their bodies, except about the anus, and pudenda. Their dugs hung between their fore-feet, and often reached almost to the ground as they walked. The hair of both sexes was of several colours, brown, red, black, and yellow. Upon the whole, I never beheld in all my travels so disagreeable an animal, or one against which I naturally conceived so strong an antipathy. So that thinking I had seen enough, full of contempt and aversion, I got up and pursued the beaten road, hoping it might direct me to the cabin of some Indian. I had not gone far when I met one of these creatures full in my way, and coming up directly to me. The ugly monster, when he saw me, distorted several ways every feature of his visage, and stared as at an object he had never seen before; then approaching nearer, lifted up his forepaw, whether out of curiosity or mischief, I could not tell. But I drew my hanger, and gave him a good blow with the flat side of it, for I durst not strike him with the edge, fearing the inhabitants might be provoked against me, if they should come to know that I had killed or maimed any of their cattle. When the beast felt the smart, he drew back, and roared so loud, that a herd of at least forty came flocking about me from the next field, howling and making odious faces; but I ran to the body of a tree, and leaning

my back against it, kept them off, by waving my hanger.
Gulliver's Travels, IV, vi

Gulliver's descriptive style is direct and factual; he is describing without preconceptions, and with the accuracy of a conscientious explorer, a species of animal hitherto unknown to him. But even so he cannot help expressing the immediate antipathy he felt for these creatures. As we read the passage we (though not yet Gulliver) gradually realise that what he is describing is a gross and bestial version of the human body, unrecognised by the describer and so seen as if for the first time. Not recognising a connection between the Yahoos and himself, Gulliver makes no attempt to hide their physical repulsiveness, which is also a moral repulsiveness. The passage is a good example of the dominant aim of satire—to make us see ourselves, or certain aspects of ourselves, afresh, as though we have never seen them before.

In the first paragraph above, Gulliver's account of how he happened to land in this strange country sounds so accurate and factual that we accept it at its face value and so go on to accept the description that follows. Examine Gulliver's style, and the kind of detail he provides, in this paragraph to see how the effect of accuracy and credibility is obtained.

Analyse the means by which the reader is slowly made aware that the Yahoo shape is a degraded and bestial version of his own. Does the gradualness of the process add to the reader's sense of shocked surprise?

Satiric use of apparently straightforward exposition

In this political pamphlet, which was widely read and influential, Swift was endeavouring on behalf of Queen Anne's Tory ministry to turn public opinion against the long war with France, in which Marlborough, with the support of the Whigs, had won spectacular victories.

3

If the Peace be made this Winter, we are then to consider, what Circumstances we shall be in towards paying a Debt of about Fifty Millions, which is a fourth Part of the Purchase of the whole Island, if it were to be Sold.

Towards clearing our selves of this monstrous Incumbrance, some of these Annuities will expire or pay off the Principal in Thirty, Forty, or a Hundred Years; the Bulk of the Debt must be lessened gradually by the best Management we can, out of what will remain of the Land and Malt Taxes, after paying Guards and Garrisons, and maintaining and supplying our Fleet in the time of Peace. I have not Skill enough to compute what will be left, after these necessary Charges, towards annually clearing so vast a Debt; but believe it must be very little: However, it is plain that both these Taxes must be continued, as well for supporting the Government, as because we have no other Means for paying off the Principal. And so likewise must all the other Funds remain for paying the Interest. How long a time this must require, how steddy an Administration, and how undisturbed a state of Affairs, both at Home and Abroad, let others determine.

However, some People think all this very reasonable, and that since the Struggle hath been for Peace and Safety, Posterity, who is to partake the Benefit, ought to share in the Expence: As if at the breaking out of this War there had been such a Conjuncture of Affairs, as never happened before, nor would ever happen again. 'Tis wonderful, that our Ancestors, in all their Wars, should never fall under such a Necessity; that we meet no Examples of it, in *Greece* and *Rome*; that no other Nation in *Europe* ever knew any thing like it, except *Spain*, about an Hundred and twenty Years ago; which they drew upon themselves, by their own Folly, and have suffered for it ever since: No doubt, we shall teach Posterity Wisdom, but they will be apt to think the Purchase too dear; and I wish they may stand to the Bargain we have made in their Names.

'Tis easy to entail Debts on succeeding Ages, and to hope they will be able and willing to pay them; but how to insure Peace for any Term of Years, is difficult enough to apprehend. Will Human Nature ever cease to have the same Passions? Princes to entertain Designs of Interest or Ambition, and Occasions of Quarrel to arise? May not we Ourselves, by the variety of Events and Incidents which happen in the World, be under a necessity of recovering Towns out of the very Hands of those, for whom we are now ruining Our Country to Take them? Neither can it be said, that those *States*, with whom we may probably differ, will be in as bad a Condition as Ourselves; for, by the Circumstances of our Situation, and the Impositions of our Allies, we are more exhausted, than either they or the Enemy; and by the Nature of our Government, the Corruption of our Manners, and the Opposition of Factions, we shall be more slow in recovering.

It will, no doubt, be a mighty Comfort to our Grandchildren, when they see a few Rags hang up in *Westminster-Hall*, which cost an hundred Millions, whereof they are paying the Arrears, and boasting, as Beggars do, that their Grandfathers were Rich and Great.

The Conduct of the Allies

The style is casual and informal, and the tone eminently reasonable; but this quiet expository manner admirably serves Swift's real purpose, which is to insinuate into the minds of his readers the idea that a weight of taxation is being laid on the country, even to future generations, only to enrich a few men who benefit financially from the war. Quiet discussion is reinforced by the impression given in the third paragraph of the author as a man sitting in his study, looking without bias through his history books for a parallel to his country's present conduct, and finding none. The wastefulness and pointlessness of the long war is further developed in the fourth paragraph : can a war however expensive establish peace (we are asked to consider) when human nature is so unlikely to change?

Thus the waste of war is set before us, inconspicuously and reasonably, from different aspects, until Swift judges us to be ready for the sudden stroke which will shock us into complete awareness. His readers' ruined grandchildren, still paying in the third generation for their ancestors' war, will surely find it worth while, he says ironically, when they see what their money has bought, 'when they see a few Rags hang up in *Westminster-Hall*, which cost an hundred Millions'. The tattered military standards, hanging in the nation's shrine as relics of great victories, are seen not as symbols of valour and conquest but as they

18

physically are—a few useless rags. Thus in a phrase we see the symbols of the glory and heroism of war turn before our eyes to a symbol of the waste and destruction of war. Again a new perspective is skilfully thrust upon us.

In *The Drapier's Letters* Swift assumes the voice of a simple honest draper of Dublin (known by his initials as 'M.B.'), who is no politician but who does know what is going to damage his trade, and does know injustice and tyranny when he sees it. The Drapier is angered by the English government's attempt to force a supply of small copper coins on the parliament and people of Ireland, against their will and to their probable detriment. The patent for coining and distributing 'Wood's halfpence' had been granted to the English entrepreneur William Wood, and the whole transaction, which involved the passing of bribes, was unsavoury. As Swift, with other Irish and Anglo-Irish leaders, saw it, the wishes, the welfare, and the dignity of the whole people of Ireland were being cynically sacrificed for the sake of some quick money-making by favourites of the king and the chief minister, Walpole.

4

Brethren, Friends, Countrymen, and Fellow-Subjects.

What I intend now to say to you, is, next to your duty to God, and the care of your salvation, of the greatest concern to your selves and your children; your bread and clothing, and every common necessary of life entirely depend upon it. Therefore I do most earnestly exhort you as men, as Christians, as parents, and as lovers of your country, to read this paper with the utmost attention, or get it read to you by others; which that you may do at the less expense, I have ordered the printer to sell it at the lowest rate.

It is a great fault among you, that when a person writes with no other intention than to do you good, you will not be at the pains to read his advices: one copy of this paper may serve a dozen of you, which will be less than a farthing apiece. It is your folly that you have no common or general interest in your view, not even the wisest among you, neither do you know or inquire, or care who are your friends, or who are your enemies.

About four years ago a little book was written, to advise all people to wear the manufactures of this our own dear country. It had no other design, said nothing against the king or parliament, or any person whatsoever; yet the poor printer was prosecuted two years with the utmost violence, and even some weavers themselves, for whose sake it was written, being upon the jury, found him guilty. This would be enough to discourage any man from endeavoring to do you good, when you will either neglect him, or fly in his face for his pains; and when he must expect only danger to himself, and to be fined and imprisoned, perhaps to his ruin.

However, I cannot but warn you once more of the manifest destruction before your eyes, if you do not behave yourselves as you ought.

I will therefore first tell you the plain story of the fact; and then I will lay before you how you ought to act in common prudence, and according to the laws of your country.

The fact is thus, it having been many years since copper halfpence or farthings were last coined in this kingdom, they have been for some time very scarce, and many counterfeits passed about under the name of raps: several applications were made to England, that we might have liberty to coin new ones, as in former times we did; but they did not succeed. At last one Mr. Wood, a mean ordinary man, a hardware dealer, procured a patent under his Majesty's broad seal to coin £108,000 in copper for this kingdom; which patent, however, did not oblige anyone here to take them, unless they pleased. Now you must know, that the halfpence and farthings in England pass for very little more than they are worth; and if you should beat them to pieces, and sell them to the brazier, you would not lose much above a penny in a shilling. But Mr. Wood made his halfpence of such base metal, and so much smaller than the English ones, that the brazier would not give you above a penny of good money for a shilling of his; so that this sum of £108,000 in good gold and silver, must be given for trash, that will not be worth above eight or nine thousand pounds real value. But this is not the worst; for Mr. Wood, when he pleases, may by stealth send over another £108,000 and buy all our goods for eleven parts in twelve under the value. For example, if a hatter sells a dozen of hats for five shillings apiece, which amounts to three pounds, and receives the payment in Mr. Wood's coin, he really receives only the value of five shillings.

Perhaps you will wonder how such an ordinary fellow as this Mr. Wood could have so much interest as to get his Majesty's broad seal for so great a sum of bad money to be sent to this poor country; and that all the nobility and gentry here could not obtain the same favour, and let us make our own halfpence, as we used to do. Now I will make that matter very plain. We are at a great distance from the king's court, and have nobody there to solicit for us, although a great number of lords and squires, whose estates are here, and are our countrymen, spend all their lives and fortunes there. But this same Mr. Wood was able to attend constantly for his own interest; he is an Englishman, and had great friends; and it seems knew very well where to give money to those that would speak to others that could speak to the king, and would tell a fair story. And his Majesty, and perhaps the great lord or lords who advised him, might think it was for our country's good; and so, as the lawyers express it, the king was deceived in his grant, which often happens in all reigns. And I am sure if his Majesty knew that such a patent, if it should take effect according to the desire of Mr. Wood, would utterly ruin this kingdom, which hath given such great proofs of its loyalty, he would immediately recall it, and perhaps show his displeasure to somebody or other: but a word to the wise is enough. Most of you must have heard with what anger our honorable House of Commons received an account of this Wood's patent. There were several fine speeches made upon it, and plain proofs, that it was all a wicked cheat from the bottom to the top; and several smart votes were printed, which that same Wood had the assurance to answer likewise in print; and in so confident a way, as if he were a better man than our whole parliament put together.

This Wood, as soon as his patent was passed, or soon after, sends over a great many barrels of those halfpence to Cork and other seaport towns; and to get them off, offered a hundred pounds in his coin for seventy or eighty in silver: but the collectors of the king's customs very honestly refused to take them, and so did almost everybody else. And since the parliament hath condemned them, and desired the king that they might be stopped, all the kingdom do abominate them.

But Wood is still working underhand to force his half-pence upon us; and if he can by help of his friends in England prevail so far as to get an order that the commissioners and collectors of the king's money shall receive them, and that the army is to be paid with them, then he thinks his work shall be done. And this is the difficulty you will be under in such a case; for the common soldier, when he goes to the market or alehouse, will offer this money; and if it be refused, perhaps he will swagger and hector, and threaten to beat the butcher or alewife, or take the goods by force and throw them the bad halfpence. In this and the like cases, the shopkeeper or victualer, or any other tradesman, has no more to do, than to demand ten

22

times the price of his goods, if it is to be paid in Wood's money: for example, twenty pence of that money for a quart of ale, and so in all things else, and not part with his goods till he gets the money.

For suppose you go to an alehouse with that base money, and the landlord gives you a quart for four of these half-pence, what must the victualer do? His brewer will not be paid in that coin, or, if the brewer should be such a fool, the farmers will not take it from them for their bere, because they are bound, by their leases, to pay their rents in good and lawful money of England, which this is not, nor of Ireland neither; and the squire, their landlord, will never be so bewitched to take such trash for his land; so that it must certainly stop somewhere or other; and wherever it stops it is the same thing, and we are all undone.

> *The Drapier's Letters: First Letter, To The*
> *Shopkeepers, Tradesmen, Farmers, and Common*
> *People of Ireland*

In order to rouse the united opposition of the people, Swift wrote his series of letters, addressed to different persons of different walks of life in Ireland. The first is addressed to people like the Drapier, or Draper, himself; and the pose of the down-to-earth tradesman, with no literary skill but with much common sense, and an honest man's disgust at sharp trading practice, enables Swift to appeal, at the level of common decency and fairness, and the necessity for making a living, to those who had no knowledge of economic theory and constitutional right. The Drapier begins with some solemnity, addressing his fellow countrymen as his brothers and friends, and presenting the opposition to Wood's halfpence as a matter of survival and also of moral duty. All differences must be forgotten in the face of so great a common danger, and the people must act as one, trusting each other like 'Brethren, Friends, Countrymen, and Fellow-Subjects'. Swift had found it difficult, over the years, to persuade the people to take a firm and united stand in their own interest, and the second and third paragraphs refer to his previous failures (and perhaps hint that the modest Drapier is really the great Dean of St. Patrick's), but the letters were successful, and the patent had to be withdrawn.

Swift's skilful use of the 'Drapier' persona reduces complicated financial issues to those simple terms of daily buying and selling which his readers will understand.

How is the simple expository style used to imply that England is setting *one* Englishman above the welfare of the whole people of Ireland, that bribery has taken place, etc.? How is it used to reduce the rich Wood to a level (that of a rather shady tradesman) at which the people can feel they can oppose him?

Satiric use of apparently straightforward argument

This short tract satirises those 'nominal Christians', Christians in name only, who call themselves believers and who take advantage of various social and other conveniences which the established church, the Church of England, provides, without allowing Christianity to impinge upon their comfort or to influence their actions. It is, in its most exactly topical aspect, an attack on those Whigs who wished to alter the laws in order to allow Dissenters and Catholics to take civil and political office; but it goes beyond this limited aim, to expose the human propensity to let matters of spiritual and moral importance become merely matters of personal convenience.

5

I am very sensible what a weakness and presumption it is to reason against the general humour and disposition of the world. I remember it was with great justice, and a due regard to the freedom both of the public and the press, forbidden upon severe penalties to write, or discourse, or lay wagers against the *Union*, even before it was confirmed by parliament, because that was looked upon as a design to oppose the current of the people, which, besides the folly of it, is a manifest breach of the fundamental law that makes this majority of opinion the voice of God. In like manner, and for the very same reasons, it may perhaps be neither safe nor prudent to argue against the abolishing of Christianity at a juncture when all parties appear so unanimously determined upon the point, as we cannot but allow from their actions, their discourses, and their writings. However, I know not how, whether from the affectation of singularity or the perverseness of human nature, but so it unhappily falls out that I cannot be entirely of this opinion. Nay, although I were sure an order were issued out for my immediate prosecution by the Attorney-General, I should still confess that in the present posture of our affairs at home or abroad, I do not yet see the absolute necessity of extirpating the Christian religion from among us.

This perhaps may appear too great a paradox even for our wise and paradoxical age to endure; therefore I shall handle it with all tenderness, and with the utmost deference to that great and profound majority which is of another sentiment.

And yet the curious may please to observe, how much the genius of a nation is liable to alter in half an age. I have heard it affirmed for certain by some very old people, that the contrary opinion was even in their memories as much in vogue as the other is now; and, that a project for the abolishing of Christianity would then have appeared as singular, and been thought as absurd, as it would be at this time to write or discourse in its defence.

Therefore I freely own that all appearances are against me. The system of the Gospel, after the fate of other systems, is generally antiquated and exploded; and the mass or body of the common people, among whom it seems to have had its latest credit, are now grown as much ashamed of it as their betters; opinion like fashions always descending from those of quality to the middle sort, and thence to the vulgar, where at length they are dropped and vanish.

But here I would not be mistaken, and must therefore be so bold as to borrow a distinction from the writers on the other side when they make a difference between nominal and real Trinitarians. I hope no reader imagines me so weak to stand up in the defence of real Christianity, such as used in primitive times (if we may believe the authors of those ages) to have an influence upon men's belief and actions : to offer at the restoring of that would indeed be a wild project; it would be to dig up foundations; to destroy at one blow all the wit and half the learning of the kingdom; to break the entire frame and constitution of things; to ruin trade, extinguish arts and sciences with the professors of them; in short, to turn our courts, exchanges, and shops into deserts; and would be full as absurd as the proposal of Horace, where he advises the Romans all in a body to leave their city and seek a new seat in some remote part of the world by way of cure for the corruption of their manners.

Therefore I think this caution was in itself altogether unnecessary, (which I have inserted only to prevent all possibility of cavilling) since every candid reader will easily understand my discourse to be intended only in defence of nominal Christianity; the other having been for some time wholly laid aside by general consent, as utterly inconsistent with our present schemes of wealth and power.

But why we should therefore cast off the name and title of Christians, although the general opinion and resolution be so violent for it, I confess I cannot (with submission) apprehend the consequence necessary. However, since the undertakers propose such wonderful advantages to the nation by this project, and advance many plausible objections against the system of Christianity, I shall briefly consider the strength of both, fairly allow them their greatest

27

weight, and offer such answers as I think most reasonable. After which I will beg leave to show what inconvenience may possibly happen by such an innovation in the present posture of our affairs. . . .

It is likewise urged that there are, by computation, in this kingdom above ten thousand parsons, whose revenues added to those of my lords the bishops would suffice to maintain at least two hundred young gentlemen of wit and pleasure, and free-thinking, enemies to priestcraft, narrow principles, pedantry, and prejudices; who might be an ornament to the Court and Town: and then, again, so great a number of able (bodied) divines might be a recruit to our fleet and armies. This indeed appears to be a consideration of some weight: but then, on the other side, several things deserve to be considered likewise: as, first, whether it may not be thought necessary that in certain tracts of country, like what we call parishes, there should be one man at least of abilities to read and write. Then it seems a wrong computation that the revenues of the Church throughout this island would be large enough to maintain two hundred young gentlemen, or even half that number, after the present refined way of living; that is, to allow each of them such a rent, as in the modern form of speech, would make them easy. But still there is in this project a greater mischief behind; and we ought to beware of the woman's folly who killed the hen that every morning laid her a golden egg. For, pray what would become of the race of men in the next age, if we had nothing to trust to besides the scrofulous, consumptive productions, furnished by our men of wit and pleasure, when having squandered away their vigour, health and estates, they are forced by some disagreeable marriage to piece up their broken fortunes, and entail rottenness and politeness on their posterity? Now, here are ten thousand persons reduced by the wise regulations of Henry the Eighth, to the necessity of a low diet, and moderate exercise, who are the only great restorers of our breed, without which the

28

nation would in an age or two become but one great
hospital.

Another advantage proposed by the abolishing of Christianity is the clean gain of one day in seven, which is now
entirely lost, and consequently the kingdom one seventh
less considerable in trade, business, and pleasure; beside
the loss to the public of so many stately structures now in
the hands of the Clergy, which might be converted into
theatres, exchanges, market-houses, common dormitories,
and other public edifices.

I hope I shall be forgiven a hard word, if I call this a
perfect cavil. I readily own there has been an old custom
time out of mind for people to assemble in the churches
every Sunday, and that shops are still frequently shut, in
order as it is conceived, to preserve the memory of that
ancient practice, but how this can prove a hindrance to
business or pleasure is hard to imagine. What if the men
of pleasure are forced one day in the week to game at
home instead of the chocolate-house? Are not the taverns
and coffeehouses open? Can there be a more convenient
season for taking a dose of physic? Are fewer claps got
upon Sundays than other days? Is not that the chief day
for traders to sum up the accounts of the week, and for
lawyers to prepare their briefs, But I would fain know how
it can be pretended that the churches are misapplied?
Where are most appointments and rendezvouzes of gal-
lantry, Where more care to appear in the foremost box
with greater advantage of dress, Where more meetings for
business? Where more bargains driven of all sorts?

An Argument against Abolishing Christianity

The persona here is himself frankly a nominal Christian,
who is naïve enough to put into words what he assumes,
from the way people talk and act, that they all think.
He assumes that everyone agrees with him in having no
sort of belief in 'The system of the Gospel' and that many

see no point in keeping it up at all. His argument is directed, therefore, against what he takes to be the majority opinion —that Christianity should be abolished—and he expects to be thought very odd and 'paradoxical' in arguing thus. The *direction* of his argument is therefore in itself an excellent satiric comment on the state of religious belief and practice, and his apologetic tone, as he prepares us for the expression of an opinion he knows to be eccentric, gives an added turn. His manner is fussy and flustered because he feels he is bound to meet with opposition and ridicule; none the less he bravely puts forward his arguments, which are of a kind which further show up his inability, and that of the other 'nominal Christians', to understand the nature of religious belief, and which emphasise the opportunistic attitude he stands for. For example, certain Christian institutions, like the keeping of Sunday, enable business and the professions to be better and more comfortably conducted. It has been said that the *Argument* supports Christianity for all the wrong reasons, thus suggesting that religion is only made use of, is no longer a faith but a practical convenience.

Examine the first three paragraphs closely to see how Swift uses the persona's apologetic sense that his news will be unpopular and may bring unpleasant consequences, to lead up to the words 'The system of the Gospel, after the fate of other systems, is generally antiquated and exploded'. The persona is hastening to explain that he agrees with the general opinion that Christianity is out of date, but that none the less he feels that, though 'exploded' it is still convenient. What is the effect of the use of the word 'system' to apply to Christianity?

Define 'real' and 'nominal' Christianity as seen in the *Argument*.

The direction of the persona's discussion is carefully

chosen to enable Swift to make, as well as his general point, some incidental satiric comments about the stipends of clergymen, the lives and education of well-to-do young men, the behaviour of people in church, and so on. Analyse the ways in which these points are made.

Parody of a style for satiric purpose

A Tale of a Tub is the most hilarious and the most difficult and complicated of all Swift's works. The allegorical narrative of the churches is interspersed with 'Digressions' in which the satire of 'abuses in learning' is contained. The persona, or pretended author, of the *Tale*, like Gulliver and other satiric masks or personae adopted by Swift, is himself the object of satire. His rambling, breathless, high-flown style, expressive of his rambling mind and inability to think clearly and consecutively, enables Swift to present a much fuller, funnier, and more persuasive picture of the comical delusions and absurdities to which the human mind is subject, than if he had merely described such things in his own voice and manner. In the *Tale*, we see them in action, not simply described or attacked.

6

We whom the world is pleased to honor with the title of modern authors, should never have been able to compass our great design of an everlasting remembrance, and never-dying fame, if our endeavours had not been so highly serviceable to the general good of mankind. This, O universe, is the adventurous attempt of me thy secretary:

—— Quemvis perferre laborem
Suadet, & inducit noctes vigilare serenas.

To this end, I have some time since, with a world of pains and art, dissected the carcass of human nature, and read many useful lectures upon the several parts, both containing and contained; till at last it smelt so strong, I could preserve it no longer. Upon which, I have been at a great expense to fit up all the bones with exact contexture, and in due symmetry; so that I am ready to show a very complete anatomy thereof to all curious gentlemen and others. But not to digress farther in the midst of a digression, as I have known some authors enclose digressions in one another, like a nest of boxes; I do affirm, that having carefully cut up human nature, I have found a very strange, new, and important discovery, that the public good of mankind is performed by two ways, instruction and diversion. And I have farther proved in my said several readings (which perhaps the world may one day see, if I can prevail on any friend to steal a copy, or on certain gentlemen of my admirers to be very importunate) that as mankind is now disposed, he receives much greater advantage by being diverted than instructed; his epidemical diseases being fastidiosity, amorphy, and oscitation; whereas in the present universal empire of wit and learning, there seems but little matter left for instruction. However, in compliance with a lesson of great age and authority, I have attempted carrying the point in all its heights; and accordingly throughout this divine treatise, have skilfully kneaded up both together with a layer of *utile*, and a layer of *dulce*.

When I consider how exceedingly our illustrious moderns have eclipsed the weak glimmering lights of the ancients, and turned them out of the road of all fashionable commerce, to a degree, that our choice town wits, of most

refined accomplishments, are in grave dispute, whether
there have been ever any ancients or no : in which point
we are like to receive wonderful satisfaction from the most
useful labours and lucubrations of that worthy modern, Dr.
Bentley : I say, when I consider all this, I cannot but be-
wail, that no famous modern hath ever yet attempted an
universal system in a small portable volume of all things
that are to be known, or believed, or imagined, or practised in life. I am, however, forced to acknowledge, that
such an enterprise was thought on some time ago by a
great philosopher of O. Brazile. The method he proposed
was by a certain curious receipt, a nostrum, which after
his untimely death, I found among his papers, and do here
out of my great affection to the modern learned, present
them with it, not doubting it may one day encourage some
worthy undertaker.

*You take fair correct copies, well bound in calf's skin,
and lettered at the back, of all modern bodies of arts and
sciences whatsoever, and in what language you please.
These you distil in* balneo Mariæ, *infusing* quintessence of
poppy Q.S., *together with three pints of* Lethe, *to be had
from the apothecaries. You cleanse away carefully the*
sordes *and* caput mortuum, *letting all that is volatile evap-
orate. You preserve only the first running, which is again
to be distilled seventeen times, till what remains will
amount to about two drams. This you keep in a glass vial,
hermetically sealed, for one-and-twenty days. Then you
begin your catholic treatise, taking every morning fasting
(first shaking the vial), three drops of this* elixir, *snuffing
it strongly up your nose. It will dilate itself about the brain
(where there is any) in fourteen minutes, and you immediately perceive in your head an infinite number of* abstracts,
summaries, compendiums, extracts, collections, medulas,
excerpta quædams, florilegias *and the like, all disposed into
great order, and reducible upon paper.*

I must needs own, it was by the assistance of this
arcanum, that I, though otherwise *impar*, have adventured

upon so daring an attempt, never achieved or undertaken before, but by a certain author called Homer, in whom, though otherwise a person not without some abilities, and for an ancient, of a tolerable genius, I have discovered many gross errors, which are not to be forgiven his very ashes, if, by chance any of them are left. For whereas we are assured he designed his work for a complete body of all knowledge, human, divine, political, and mechanic, it is manifest he hath wholly neglected some, and been very imperfect in the rest. For, first of all, as eminent a cabalist as his disciples would represent him, his account of the *opus magnum* is extremely poor and deficient; he seems to have read but very superficially either Sendivogius, Behmen, or *Anthroposophia Theomagica*. He is also quite mistaken about the *sphœra pyroplastica*, a neglect not to be atoned for; and (if the reader will admit so severe a censure), *vix crederem autorem hunc, unquam audivisse ignis vocem*. His failings are not less prominent in several parts of the mechanics. For, having read his writings with the utmost application usual among modern wits, I could never yet discover the least direction about the structure of that useful instrument, a save-all. For want of which, if the moderns had not lent their assistance, we might yet have wandered in the dark. But I have still behind, a fault far more notorious to tax this author with; I mean, his gross ignorance in the common laws of this realm, and in the doctrine as well as discipline of the Church of England. A defect indeed, for which both he and all the ancients stand most justly censured, by my worthy and ingenious friend, Mr. Wotton, Bachelor of Divinity, in his incomparable treatise of *Ancient and Modern Learning*, a book never to be sufficiently valued, whether we consider the happy turns and flowings of the author's wit, the great usefulness of his sublime discoveries upon the subject of flies and spittle, or the laborious eloquence of his style. And I cannot forbear doing that author the justice of my public acknowledgments, for the great helps and liftings I had out of his incomparable piece, while I was penning this treatise. . . .

It was to supply such momentous defects, that I have been prevailed on after long solicitation, to take pen in hand; and I dare venture to promise, the judicious reader shall find nothing neglected here, that can be of use upon any emergency of life. I am confident to have included and exhausted all that human imagination can rise or fall to. Particularly I recommend to the perusal of the learned certain discoveries that are wholly untouched by others; whereof I shall only mention among a great many more my *New Help of Smatterers, or the Art of being Deep-Learned and Shallow-read; A Curious Invention about Mouse-Traps; An Universal Rule of Reason, or Every Man his own Carver;* together with a most useful engine for catching owls. All which the judicious reader will find largely treated on in the several parts of this discourse.

A Tale of a Tub, Section V : 'A Digression in the
Modern Kind'

The style of the digressive parts of the *Tale* is one which Swift does not use in his own person. His personal way of writing is very concise and logically structured, very clear and easy to follow. But here he adopts an old-fashioned seventeenth-century style, wandering, circumlocutory, digressive, and metaphorical, with long sentences very loosely connected. As we read, we begin to feel that the loose digressive style is the inevitable utterance of a loosely working mind, incapable of sustained thought because too egotistical to subdue itself to hard reality. The persona proceeds not from fact to fact or thought to thought, but from image to image or impression to impression. He cannot weigh probabilities, and is ignorant of the nature of evidence; he believes what he wants to believe, especially what adds to his sense of his own importance. He cannot distinguish the relative values of the things that enter his head, or their relevance to what he has written, for all that concerns him is himself, and everything that occurs to *him* seems equally important. His way of writing expresses this perfectly. He is at great pains to insist that modern authors, of whom *he* is one, are far superior to the ancient writers of Greece and Rome. Since he looks in Homer for pieces of knowledge which are not only trivial in themselves but were non-existent in Homer's time, the persona's case is, by his own peculiar methods, easily proved to his satisfaction. Everything he writes makes more evident what Swift sees as the typically 'modern' vice of egoism and self-conceit, which must lead to delusion because it causes a man to believe his own pleasing fantasies rather than plain facts.

The most useful and instructive way to read any passage from the Digressions in the *Tale* is to analyse it very closely, clause by clause and image by image. Almost every detail contributes to the portrayal of wrongheaded absurdity. For this reason the approaches suggested below all point to such stylistic details :

Count the number of times the word 'I' occurs in this extract.

Consider the effect made, in building up the impression of self-centred muddle-headedness, by the lofty phrases of paragraph one (never-dying fame, This, O Universe . . .); the digressive style in which the persona writes about digressions in paragraph two; the pompous, repetitive, long-winded sentence which opens paragraph three. The effect is heightened by the recipe in paragraph four (this expresses credulity, wishful thinking, superficiality, a desire to learn by the easy way); the references to mysterious, semi-mystical works like those of Behmen or of Thomas Vaughan, author of *Anthroposophia Theomagica* (to which Swift adds a note : 'it is a piece of the most unintelligible fustian, that, perhaps, was ever published in any language.');

clichés like 'while I was penning this treatise', 'I have been prevailed upon after long solicitation, to take pen in hand'.

7

But the greatest maim given to that general reception, which the writings of our society have formerly received (next to the transitory state of all sublunary things) hath been a superficial vein among many readers of the present age, who will by no means be persuaded to inspect beyond the surface and the rind of things; whereas wisdom is a fox, who after long hunting will at last cost you the pains to dig out. 'Tis a cheese, which by how much the richer, has the thicker, the homelier, and the coarser coat; and whereof to a judicious palate, the maggots are the best. 'Tis a sack-posset, wherein the deeper you go, you will find it the sweeter. Wisdom is a hen, whose cackling we must value and consider, because it is attended with an egg. But then lastly, 'tis a nut, which unless you choose with judgment, may cost you a tooth, and pay you with nothing but a worm. In consequence of these momentous truths, the Grubæan Sages have always chosen to convey their precepts and their arts, shut up within the vehicles of types and fables, which having been perhaps more careful and curious in adorning, than was altogether necessary, it has fared with these vehicles after the usual fate of coaches over-finely painted and gilt, that the transitory gazers have so dazzled their eyes, and filled their imaginations with the outward lustre, as neither to regard or consider the person or the parts of the owner within. A misfortune we undergo with somewhat less reluctancy, because it has been common to us with Pythagoras, Æsop, Socrates, and other of our predecessors.

A Tale of a Tub, Introduction

The persona here attempts to prove that the popular journalism of the seventeenth and eighteenth centuries (called 'Grub Street' writing) is not mere ephemeral catch-penny stuff but—if its readers were intelligent enough to perceive it—profound allegory. All wisdom worth finding, he says, is concealed; and to prove this by analogy he launches upon a string of metaphors, one suggesting another; but somehow all his metaphors have certain unfortunate connotations which suggest the opposite of what he intends. Wisdom is a fox; a cheese, which is all the better for having maggots in it; a posset, or sweet drink, where the sweetness is at the bottom; a hen, whose cackling sounds foolish but is after all 'attended with an egg', and at last, in a hopelessly inept metaphor, wisdom is a nut, which takes a lot of cracking and which, unless you choose it carefully, may break your tooth and give you only a worm-eaten kernel in exchange. The persona's metaphorical style is so uncontrolled and fanciful that it proves that the 'wisdom' hidden in the profound works of Grub Street authors like himself is not worth the misery of reading their books—not at all what he means to show. The ineptitude of his mind, and the minds of those he supports, is again excellently embodied in his way of writing.

8

And whereas the mind of Man, when he gives the spur and bridle to his thoughts, doth never stop, but naturally sallies out into both extremes of high and low, of good and evil; his first flight of fancy commonly transports him to ideas of what is most perfect, finished and exalted; till having soared out of his own reach and sight, not well perceiving how near the frontiers of height and depth border upon each other; with the same course and wing, he falls down plumb into the lowest bottom of things, like one who travels the east into the west, or like a straight line drawn by its own length into a circle. Whether a tincture of malice in our natures makes us fond of furnishing every bright idea with its reverse; or whether reason, reflecting upon the sum of things, can, like the sun, serve only to enlighten one half of the globe, leaving the other half, by necessity, under shade and darkness; or, whether fancy, flying up to the imagination of what is highest and best, becomes over-shot, and spent, and weary, and suddenly falls like a dead bird of paradise to the ground. Or whether after all these metaphysical conjectures, I have not entirely missed the true reason; the proposition, however, which has stood me in so much circumstance, is altogether true; that, as the most uncivilized parts of mankind have some way or other climbed up into the conception of a God, or Supreme Power, so they have seldom forgot to provide their fears with certain ghastly notions, which, instead of better, have served them pretty tolerably for a devil.

A Tale of a Tub, Section VIII

The persona here ambitiously attempts to account for certain propensities in the human mind, which cause it, having come to the conception of a benevolent god, to come also to the conception of a devil. His own mind 'sallies out' into this difficult task, which is altogether beyond his powers. Caught up by his own metaphor, he is carried by it instead of bending it to his own purposes, and his long breathless sentences and his images of flying and falling, of a straight line 'drawn by its own length into a circle', and finally of the bird of paradise, whose aimless and unproductive flight ends in an ignominious flop to the ground, perfectly express the ambitious but directionless flight of his own mind, which (as he begins dimly to suspect) may after all have entirely missed the point,

'the true reason'. The style of this extract should be ana-
lysed in detail, along the lines suggested above.

9

Nothing but an extreme love of truth could have hindered
me from concealing this part of my story. It was in vain
to discover my resentments, which were always turned
into ridicule; and I was forced to rest with patience while
my noble and most beloved country was so injuriously
treated. I am heartily sorry as any of my readers can possibly be, that such an occasion was given : but this prince
happened to be so curious and inquisitive upon every particular, that it could not consist either with gratitude or
good manners to refuse giving him what satisfaction I was
able. Yet thus much I may be allowed to say in my own
vindication, that I artfully eluded many of his questions,
and gave to every point a more favourable turn by many
degrees than the strictness of truth would allow. For I have
always borne that laudable partiality to my own country,
which Dionysius Halicarnassensis with so much justice
recommends to an historian. I would hide the frailties and
deformities of my political mother, and place her virtues
and beauties in the most advantageous light. This was my
sincere endeavour in those many discourses I had with that
mighty monarch, although it unfortunately failed of
success.

But great allowances should be given to a king who lives
wholly secluded from the rest of the world, and must therefore be altogether unacquainted with the manners and customs that most prevail in other nations : the want of which
knowledge will ever produce many prejudices, and a certain narrowness of thinking, from which we and the politer
countries of Europe are wholly exempted. And it would
be hard indeed, if so remote a prince's notions of virtue
and vice were to be offered as a standard for all mankind.

To confirm what I have now said, and further to show the miserable effects of a confined education, I shall here insert a passage which will hardly obtain belief. In hopes to ingratiate my self farther into his Majesty's favour, I told him of an invention discovered between three and four hundred years ago, to make a certain powder, into an heap of which the smallest spark of fire falling, would kindle the whole in a moment, although it were as big as a mountain, and make it all fly up in the air together, with a noise and agitation greater than thunder. That a proper quantity of this powder rammed into an hollow tube of brass or iron, according to its bigness, would drive a ball of iron or lead with such violence and speed as nothing was able to sustain its force. That the largest balls, thus discharged, would not only destroy whole ranks of any army at once, but batter the strongest walls to the ground, sink down ships, with a thousand men in each, to the bottom of the sea; and when linked together by a chain, would cut through masts and rigging, divide hundreds of bodies in the middle, and lay all waste before them. That we often put this powder into large hollow balls of iron, and discharged them by an engine into some city we were besieging, which would rip up the pavement, tear the houses to pieces, burst and throw splinters on every side, dashing out the brains of all who came near. That I knew the ingredients very well, which were cheap, and common; I understood the manner of compounding them, and could direct his workmen how to make those tubes of a size proportionable to all other things in his Majesty's kingdom, and the largest need not be above two hundred foot long; twenty or thirty of which tubes, charged with the proper quantity of powder and balls, would batter down the walls of the strongest town in his dominions in a few hours, or destroy the whole metropolis, if ever it should pretend to dispute his absolute commands. This I humbly offered to his Majesty as a small tribute of acknowledgment in return of so many marks that I had received of his royal favour and protection.

The King was struck with horror at the description I had given of those terrible engines, and the proposal I had made. He was amazed how so impotent and groveling an insect as I (these were his expressions) could entertain such inhuman ideas, and in so familiar a manner as to appear wholly unmoved at all the scenes of blood and desolation, which I had painted as the common effects of those destructive machines, whereof he said, some evil genius, enemy to mankind, must have been the first contriver. As for himself, he protested, that although few things delighted him so much as new discoveries in art or in nature, yet he would rather lose half his kingdom than be privy to such a secret, which he commanded me, as I valued my life, never to mention any more.

A strange effect of narrow principles and short views! that a prince possessed of every quality which procures veneration, love, and esteem; of strong parts, great wisdom and profound learning, endued with admirable talents for government, and almost adored by his subjects, should from a nice unnecessary scruple, whereof in Europe we can have no conception, let slip an opportunity put into his hands, that would have made him absolute master of the lives, the liberties, and the fortunes of his people. Neither do I say this with the least intention to detract from the many virtues of that excellent king, whose character I am sensible will on this account be very much lessened in the opinion of an English reader : but I take this defect among them to have risen from their ignorance, by not having hitherto reduced politics into a science, as the more acute wits of Europe have done. For I remember very well, in a discourse one day with the King, when I happened to say there were several thousand books among us written upon the art of government, it gave him (directly contrary to my intention) a very mean opinion of our understandings. He professed both to abominate and despise all mystery, refinement, and intrigue, either in a prince or a minister. He could not tell what I meant by secrets of state, where an enemy or some rival nation were not in the case. He confined the knowledge of governing within very narrow bounds; to common sense and reason, to justice and lenity, to the speedy determination of civil and criminal causes; with some other obvious topics which are not worth considering. And he gave it for his opinion, that whoever could make two ears of corn, or two blades of grass to grow upon a spot of ground where only one grew before, would deserve better of mankind, and do more essential service to his country, than the whole race of politicians put together.

Gulliver's Travels, II, vii

Gulliver, on his second voyage, finds himself in Brobdingnag, the land of the giants. The giant king is a compassionate man and a good, just ruler, and when Gulliver tells him, with some pride, of the political, social, and other institutions of England and Europe he is dismayed at what he hears. Gulliver's pride in himself and in his country because it is *his* country, is badly shaken by his tiny size in the land of giants; for the most part they are kind to him, but they treat him as a pet, which he feels detrimental to his dignity. The king's sorrowful disapproval of those customs of his native land of which he is so proud, further demoralises him; and in an attempt to win the king's approval and envy he reveals to him the greatest and proudest achievement of European man—the invention of gunpowder. Trying to impress the king and put him in his debt, Gulliver even offers to tell him how to make gunpowder, and thus to make himself supreme in power over his subjects

Gulliver's way of writing here, as he recounts his conversations with the good king, is markedly complacent and condescending. His shaken pride forbids him to see the moral excellence of the king's horror at what he has

44

been told; instead, he sneers at the king's provinciality and lack of political sophistication, regretting his narrowness of mind. With the same complacency he describes, with the utmost vividness, the carnage caused by cannon balls. Vividly as he visualises these scenes, he is not in the least affected by their horror (as the king points out, in dismay at his ruthlessness) but regards them with pride. Gulliver's pomposity, lack of feeling, complacent amusement at the king's lack of political acumen, are all expressed in his way of writing; and they suggest man's readiness to become accustomed to wrong, to cruelty, if it is in his interest to do so. Gulliver's account shows us, in its revelation of the responses of this representative human being, how easily we blind ourselves, by national pride, by excuses of political necessity, and so on, to the immorality and cruelty of our actions as individuals or as nations.

Note also, in this passage, that the standards of government of the giant king ('A strange effect of narrow principles and short views!' says Gulliver smugly) are all of a moral and practical nature. Governing, to him, means establishing justice and seeing that there is enough food for all—growing two ears of corn where one grew before. It has nothing to do with power politics, a matter of which he knows, and wishes to know, nothing.

Show, by detailed examination of Gulliver's choice of words and framing of sentences, how his way of writing betrays *himself*, not the king, as being prejudiced and narrow. Note especially how he has come to substitute clichés for thought, and is out of touch with reality: his catch words of 'prejudices', 'narrowness of thinking', 'a nice unnecessary scruple', protect him from facing unpleasing facts about himself and his country.

Parody of a form for satiric purpose

As he will use parody of a style to present, ironically, an attitude of mind, so will Swift use parody of a literary form. Thus in *Gulliver's Travels* he exploits, for satiric effect, the literature of travel, using the accounts of new countries and peoples of Europe. *A Tale of a Tub* is a story almost swamped by chapters headed 'Digression' and dealing with a variety of subjects. The most brazen title, and the most frankly irrelevant material, are those of 'A Digression in Praise of Digressions', for here the author, far from trying to make his material seem relevant to the narrative of the three brothers, shows himself quite openly and complacently as trying to spin out what he has to say to make a book of publishable and profitable length by 'transcribing from others, and digressing from himself'. The *Tale* becomes itself an example of what Swift is satirising, the 'modern' tendency to think that whatever concerns one's self is important enough to write down. An extreme example of this tendency is the Grub Street hack writer's willingness to put down anything to cover the necessary number of pages. Any rational criterion of relevance is lost, for to the author anything is relevant if it comes into

46

his head (*he* is the only criterion). The form of the *Tale*, in which digressions swallow up the story, is a *reductio ad absurdum* of a journalistic tendency.

10

I have sometimes heard of an *Iliad* in a nutshell; but it hath been my fortune to have much oftener seen a nutshell in an *Iliad*. There is no doubt that human life has received most wonderful advantages from both; but to which of the two the world is chiefly indebted, I shall leave among the curious, as a problem worthy of their utmost inquiry. For the invention of the latter, I think the commonwealth of learning is chiefly obliged to the great modern improvement of digressions: the late refinements in knowledge, running parallel to those of diet in our nation, which among men of a judicious taste are dressed up in various compounds, consisting in soups and olios, fricassees, and ragouts.

'Tis true, there is a sort of morose, detracting, ill-bred people, who pretend utterly to disrelish these polite innovations; and as to the similitude from diet, they allow the parallel, but are so bold to pronounce the example itself, a corruption and degeneracy of taste. They tell us that the fashion of jumbling fifty things together in a dish, was at first introduced in compliance to a depraved and debauched appetite, as well as to a crazy constitution: and to see a man hunting through an olio, after the head and brains of a goose, a widgeon, or a woodcock, is a sign he wants a stomach and digestion for more substantial victuals. Farther, they affirm, that digressions in a book are like foreign troops in a state, which argue the nation to want a heart and hands of its own, and often either subdue the natives, or drive them into the most unfruitful corners.

But, after all that can be objected by these supercilious censors, 'tis manifest, the society of writers would quickly be reduced to a very inconsiderable number, if men were put upon making books, with the fatal confinement of delivering nothing beyond what is to the purpose. 'Tis acknowledged, that were the case the same among us, as with the Greeks and Romans, when learning was in its cradle, to be reared and fed, and clothed by invention, it would be an easy task to fill up volumes upon particular occasions, without farther expatiating from the subject than my moderate excursions, helping to advance or clear the main design. But with knowledge it has fared as with a numerous army, encamped in a fruitful country, which for a few days maintains itself by the product of the soil it is on; till provisions being spent, they send to forage many a mile, among friends or enemies, it matters not. Meanwhile, the neighbouring fields, trampled and beaten down, become barren and dry, affording no sustenance but clouds of dust.

The whole course of things being thus entirely changed between us and the ancients, and the moderns wisely sensible of it, we of this age have discovered a shorter, and more prudent method, to become scholars and wits, without the fatigue of reading or of thinking. The most accomplished way of using books at present is two-fold: either first, to serve them as some men do lords, learn their titles exactly, and then brag of their acquaintance. Or secondly, which is indeed the choicer, the profounder, and politer method, to get a thorough insight into the index, by which the whole book is governed and turned, like fishes by the tail. For, to enter the palace of learning at the great gate, requires an expense of time and forms; therefore men of much haste and little ceremony are content to get in by the back door. For the arts are all in a flying march, and therefore more easily subdued by attacking them in the rear. Thus physicians discover the state of the whole body, by consulting only what comes from behind. Thus men catch knowledge by throwing their wit on the posteriors of a book, as boys do sparrows with flinging salt upon

48

their tails. Thus human life is best understood by the wise man's rule of regarding the end. Thus are the sciences found like Hercules's oxen, by tracing them backwards. Thus are old sciences unravelled like old stockings, by beginning at the foot.

Besides all this, the army of the sciences hath been of late, with a world of martial discipline, drawn into its close order, so that a view or a muster may be taken of it with abundance of expedition. For this great blessing we are wholly indebted to systems and abstracts, in which the modern fathers of learning, like prudent usurers, spent their sweat for the ease of us their children. For labor is the seed of idleness, and it is the peculiar happiness of our noble age to gather the fruit.

Now the method of growing wise, learned, and sublime, having become so regular an affair, and so established in all its forms, the numbers of writers must needs have increased accordingly, and to a pitch that has made it of absolute necessity for them to interfere continually with each other. Besides, it is reckoned, that there is not at this present, a sufficient quantity of new matter left in nature, to furnish and adorn any one particular subject to the extent of a volume. This I am told by a very skilful computer, who hath given a full demonstration of it from rules of arithmetic. . . . What remains therefore, but that our last recourse must be had to large indexes, and little compendiums; quotations must be plentifully gathered, and booked in alphabet; to this end, though authors need be little consulted, yet critics, and commentators, and lexicons carefully must. But above all, those judicious collectors of bright parts, and flowers, and observandas, are to be nicely dwelt on, by some called the sieves and boulters of learning, though it is left undetermined, whether they dealt in pearls or meal, and consequently, whether we are more to value that which passed through, or what stayed behind.

By these methods, in a few weeks, there starts up many a writer, capable of managing the profoundest and most universal subjects. For, what though his head be empty, provided his commonplace book be full; and if you will bate him but the circumstances of method, and style, and grammar, and invention; allow him but the common privileges of transcribing from others, and digressing from himself, as often as he shall see occasion; he will desire no more ingredients towards fitting up a treatise, that shall make a very comely figure on a bookseller's shelf; there to be preserved neat and clean for a long eternity, adorned with the heraldry of its title fairly inscribed on a label; never to be thumbed or greased by students, nor bound to everlasting chains of darkness in a library; but when the fulness of time is come, shall haply undergo the trial of purgatory, in order to ascend the sky. . . .

The necessity of this digression will easily excuse the length; and I have chosen for it as proper a place as I could readily find. If the judicious reader can assign a fitter, I do here empower him to remove it into any other corner he pleases. And so I return with great alacrity to pursue a more important concern.

> *A Tale of a Tub*, Section VII :
> 'A Digression in Praise of Digressions'

The author is, in the passage above, spinning some extra pages out of virtually nothing. He piles up images where one would serve (and incidentally, as in Extract 7, often discredits his argument by his unfortunate choice of comparison). It would be useful to make a short summary of the author's arguments to justify the practice of filling up a book with digressions (his own practice, at the moment of writing, being an example), for the summary would show clearly the absurdity of his views, and how Swift skilfully makes him condemn himself even when he supposes he is justifying himself.

Note that, in paragraphs three, four, and five Swift uses the author's justifications to expose his lack of knowledge.

The author argues that, in a late historical period like his own, it is more difficult than it used to be to become learned, and so have a sufficient store of material to suggest new ideas, and to write a book worth reading. So 'the most accomplished way' of getting some knowledge is not to read books, but to run through the indexes. And indeed the author's Digressions, patched up as they are with the names of books, with snatches of philosophy, and with Latin quotations, might well have been written by this method: they are spun out of bits and pieces.

In *A Modest Proposal* Swift parodies a particular kind of pamphlet, the straightforward argument for some particular economic policy. The words 'A Modest Proposal' frequently, in the eighteenth century, formed part of the title of such pamphlets, and Swift uses it here to underline his meaning and purpose. *His* 'Modest Proposal' is one to end all Modest Proposals; he uses parody of a form to press home the hopeless inadequacy of the usual economic theories in the face of the horrors of Ireland.

II

It is a melancholy object to those who walk through this great town, or travel in the country, when they see the streets, the roads and cabin-doors crowded with beggars of the female sex, followed by three, four, or six children, all in rags, and importuning every passenger for an alms. These mothers, instead of being able to work for their honest livelihood, are forced to employ all their time in strolling, to beg sustenance for their helpless infants, who, as they grow up, either turn thieves for want of work, or leave their dear native country to fight for the Pretender in Spain, or sell themselves to the Barbadoes.

I think it is agreed by all parties that this prodigious

number of children, in the arms, or on the backs, or at the heels of their mothers, and frequently of their fathers, is in the present deplorable state of the kingdom a very great additional grievance; and therefore whoever could find out a fair, cheap, and easy method of making these children sound and useful members of the commonwealth would deserve so well of the public as to have his statue set up for a preserver of the nation.

But my intention is very far from being confined to provide only for the children or professed beggars; it is of a much greater extent, and shall take in the whole number of infants at a certain age who are born of parents in effect as little able to support them as those who demand our charity in the streets.

As to my own part, having turned my thoughts for many years upon this important subject, and maturely weighed the several schemes of other projectors, I have always found them grossly mistaken in their computation. It is true a child just dropped from its dam may be supported by her milk for a solar year with little other nourishment, at most not above the value of two shillings, which the mother may certainly get, or the value in scraps, by her lawful occupation of begging, and it is exactly at one year old that I propose to provide for them, in such a manner as, instead of being a charge upon their parents, or the parish, or wanting food and raiment for the rest of their lives, they shall, on the contrary, contribute to the feeding and partly to the clothing of many thousands.

There is likewise another great advantage in my scheme, that it will prevent those voluntary abortions, and that horrid practice of women murdering their bastard children, alas, too frequent among us, sacrificing the poor innocent babes, I doubt, more to avoid the expense than the shame, which would move tears and pity in the most savage and inhuman breast.

The number of souls in Ireland being usually reckoned one million and a half, of these I calculate there may be about two hundred thousand couples whose wives are breeders, from which number I subtract thirty thousand couples who are able to maintain their own children, although I apprehend there cannot be so many under the present distresses of the kingdom, but this being granted, there will remain an hundred and seventy thousand breeders. I again subtract fifty thousand for those women who miscarry, or whose children die by accident or disease within the year. There only remain an hundred and twenty thousand children of poor parents annually born : the question therefore is, how this number shall be reared, and provided for, which, as I have already said, under the present situation of affairs is utterly impossible by all the methods hitherto proposed, for we can neither employ them in handicraft or agriculture; we neither build houses (I mean in the country), nor cultivate land : they can very seldom pick up a livelihood by stealing until they arrive at six years old, except where they are of towardly parts, although I confess they learn the rudiments much earlier, during which time they can however be properly looked upon only as probationers, as I have been informed by a principal gentleman in the County of Cavan, who protested to me that he never knew above one or two instances under the age of six, even in a part of the kingdom so renowned for the quickest proficiency in that art.

I am assured by our merchants that a boy or a girl before twelve years old, is no saleable commodity, and even when they come to this age, they will not yield above three pounds, or three pounds and half-a-crown at most on the Exchange, which cannot turn to account either to the parents or the kingdom, the charge of nutriment and rags having been at least four times that value.

I shall now therefore humbly propose my own thoughts, which I hope will not be liable to the least objection.

I have been assured by a very knowing American of my acquaintance in London, that a young healthy child well nursed is at a year old a most delicious, nourishing and wholesome food, whether stewed, roasted, baked, or boiled, and I make no doubt that it will equally serve in a fricassee, or a ragout.

I do therefore humbly offer it to public consideration, that of the hundred and twenty thousand children already computed, twenty thousand may be reserved for breed, whereof only one fourth part to be males, which is more than we allow to sheep, black-cattle, or swine, and my reason is that these children are seldom the fruits of marriage, a circumstance not much regarded by our savages, therefore one male will be sufficient to serve four females. That the remaining hundred thousand may at a year old be offered in sale to the persons of quality, and fortune, through the kingdom, always advising the mother to let them suck plentifully in the last month, so as to render them plump, and fat for a good table. A child will make two dishes at an entertainment for friends, and when the family dines alone, the fore or hind quarter will make a reasonable dish, and seasoned with a little pepper or salt will be very good boiled on the fourth day, especially in winter. . . .

I have already computed the charge of nursing a beggar's child (in which list I reckon all cottagers, labourers, and four-fifths of the farmers) to be about two shillings per annum, rags included, and I believe no gentleman would repine to give ten shillings for the carcass of a good fat child, which, as I have said, will make four dishes of excellent nutritive meat, when he hath only some particular friend or his own family to dine with him. Thus the Squire will learn to be a good landlord and grow popular among his tenants, the mother will have eight shillings net profit, and be fit for work until she produces another child.

Those who are more thrifty (as I must confess the times require) may flay the carcass; the skin of which artificially dressed will make admirable gloves for ladies, and summer boots for fine gentlemen. . . .

54

After all I am not so violently bent upon my own opinion as to reject any offer, proposed by wise men, which shall be found equally innocent, cheap, easy and effectual. But before some thing of that kind shall be advanced in contradiction to my scheme, and offering a better, I desire the author, or authors, will be pleased maturely to consider two points. First, as things now stand, how they will be able to find food and raiment for a hundred thousand useless mouths and backs? And secondly, there being a round million of creatures in human figure, throughout this kingdom, whose whole subsistence put into a common stock would leave them in debt two millions of pounds sterling; adding those who are beggars by profession, to the bulk of farmers, cottagers, and labourers with their wives and children, who are beggars in effect; I desire those politicians who dislike my overture, and may perhaps be so bold to attempt an answer, that they will first ask the parents of these mortals whether they would not at this day think it a great happiness to have been sold for food at a year old, in the manner I prescribe, and thereby have avoided such a perpetual scene of misfortunes as they have since gone through, by the oppression of landlords, the impossibility of paying rent without money or trade, the want of common sustenance, with neither house nor clothes to cover them from the inclemencies of weather, and the most inevitable prospect of entailing the like, or greater miseries upon their breed for ever.

A Modest Proposal for Preventing the Children of Poor People in Ireland from being a Burden to their Parents or Country and for making them Beneficial to the Public

This is perhaps the most brilliant, complex, and moving of Swift's shorter satiric pieces; the form chosen to be parodied, the persona chosen to put it forward, the details of the scheme, the calm tone in which the economist persona presents his desperate proposal, all these are calculated with the utmost precision to expose the condition of Ireland, especially of the Irish poor, and to express the cold anger of Swift himself at the miseries of the country he lived in. Essentially, the *Proposal* is an exposure of the desperate state of Ireland, exploited as it was by the English government (who refused to allow any industry or export which competed with English interests), and by the absentee landlords who neglected their Irish estates and rack-rented their tenants, and lived in England on their Irish revenues, taking no thought for their responsibilities at home. Secondarily, it is an appeal to the demoralized common people of Ireland to do what they could for themselves.

The 'proposal' put forward is perfectly chosen as a way of shocking all concerned into seeing the consequences of their actions. It is that, since all the ways in which the people of Ireland can usefully maintain themselves seem to be closed to them they should try to make money out of the only thing left—themselves. They should slaughter and market their children, as a delicate dish, at the age when it is becoming difficult to feed them—difficult because the parents are too poor to provide food. The style is extremely practical and factual; like the sound economist he is, the persona has worked out in detail the age to which children can be maintained at small cost: the number of children who can be provided for under his scheme and so can contribute to the resources of the kingdom: the money the sale of their flesh will bring in: the market there is likely to be for it: the useful and profitable by-products that will result from the flaying of the children's carcasses. One of the most devastating pieces of satire in the work is implicit in the persona's assumption that it is essential to prove that his plan is *economically* sound, and will contribute to national prosperity. No one, he

56

assumes, would listen to a scheme to relieve the sufferings of the poor on moral or humanitarian grounds. He himself accepts the primacy of economic considerations, and discusses the children in financial terms: 'the maintenance of an hundred thousand children . . . cannot be computed at less than ten shillings a piece *per annum*, the nation's stock will be thereby increased fifty thousand pounds *per annum*'. People matter only in so far as they contribute so much per head to 'the nation's stock'. Current economic theory, in Swift's time, was based on the aphorism that a country's riches consisted in its people, and that the population should, accordingly, be kept up and increased. But in Ireland the people can only contribute to their country's resources by dying; this is the measure of the unique horror of the Irish situation, where the people, with no work left for them, are an embarrassment, rather than a source of wealth, to their country. Thus the familiar form of the economic treatise is made a means of exposing the inhumanity of public policies, and private actions, which can be thought of as the result of economic theory and economic necessity; and of showing that the methods of the financier are not enough. In a final twist of the knife, Swift has his persona protest that his proposal is far from being impractical, and far from being inhumane. For what other course is left? And would not the children be better off dead than living the wretched lives their parents are forced to lead? Compared with the lives of the Irish poor, is not death at the age of one year a humane and kindly proposal? Ask the parents, says the persona; they would 'think it a great happiness to have been sold for food at a year old'.

The effect of certain words and phrases in the extract can be examined: the Irish 'leave their native country' to fight for Spain or to sell themselves as slaves; 'a beggar's child (in which list I reckon all cottagers, labourers, and four-fifths of the farmers)'.

The following phrases also deserve close study : 'her lawful occupation of begging'; children 'can very seldom pick up a livelihood by stealing until they arrive at six years old, except where they are of towardly parts'; 'Thus (by buying the slaughtered child of his tenant for dinner) the Squire will learn to be a good landlord and grow popular among his tenants, the mother will have eight shillings net profit, and be fit for work until she produces another child.'

Satiric use of imagery

The use of images for satiric purpose is of course visible in some of the extracts which follow and in some cases, though not all, attention will be drawn to it in the commentary. But Swift also, in some of his longer works, makes a more sustained use of imagery, in which a recurrent comparison subtly influences our attitude towards the events or ideas in the work, or towards the persona who writes about them. For example the author of *A Tale of a Tub*, in his Digressions, makes such frequent use of images of dissecting, flaying, reducing books or theories to skeletons, that we begin to think of him as 'murdering', reducing to nothing, any subject he chooses to write upon.

12

In about a month, when all was prepared, I sent to receive his Majesty's commands, and to take my leave. The Emperor and royal family came out of the palace; I lay down on my face to kiss his hand, which he very graciously gave me: so did the Empress, and young princes of the blood. His Majesty presented me with fifty purses of two hundred *sprugs* apiece, together with his picture at full length, which I put immediately into one of my gloves, to keep it from being hurt. The ceremonies at my departure were too many to trouble the reader with at this time.

I stored the boat with the carcasses of an hundred oxen, and three hundred sheep, with bread and drink proportionable, and as much meat ready dressed as four hundred cooks could provide. I took with me six cows and two bulls alive, with as many ewes and rams, intending to carry them into my own country, and propagate the breed. And to feed them on board, I had a good bundle of hay, and a bag of corn. I would gladly have taken a dozen of the natives, but this was a thing the Emperor would by no means permit; and besides a diligent search into my pockets, his Majesty engaged my honour not to carry away any of his subjects, although with their own consent and desire.

Gulliver's Travels, I, viii

13

I reflected what a mortification it must prove to me to appear as inconsiderable in this nation as one single Lilliputian would be among us. But this I conceived was to be the least of my misfortunes: for, as human creatures are observed to be more savage and cruel in proportion to their bulk, what could I expect but to be a morsel in the mouth of the first among these enormous barbarians who should happen to seize me? Undoubtedly philosophers are in the right when they tell us, that nothing is great or little otherwise than by comparison. It might have pleased fortune to let the Lilliputians find some nation, where the people were as diminutive with respect to them, as they were to me. And who knows but that even this prodigious race of mortals might be equally overmatched in some distant part of the world, whereof we have yet no discovery?

Scared and confounded as I was, I could not forbear going on with these reflections, when one of the reapers, approaching within ten yards of the ridge where I lay, made me apprehend that with the next step I should be squashed to death under his foot, or cut in two with his reaping hook. And therefore, when he was again about to move, I screamed as loud as fear could make me. Whereupon the huge creature trod short, and looking round about under him for some time, at last espied me as I lay on the ground. He considered a while with the caution of one who endeavours to lay hold on a small dangerous animal in such a manner that it shall not be able either to scratch or to bite him, as I my self have sometimes done with a weasel in England. At length he ventured to take me up behind by the middle between his forefinger and thumb, and brought me within three yards of his eyes, that he might behold my shape more perfectly. I guessed his meaning, and my good fortune gave me so much presence of mind, that I resolved not to struggle in the least as he held me in the air above sixty foot from the ground, although he grievously pinched my sides, for fear I should slip through his fingers. All I ventured was to raise my eyes towards the sun, and place my hands together in a supplicating posture, and to speak some words in an humble melancholy tone, suitable to the condition I then was in. For I apprehended every moment that he would dash me against the ground, as we usually do any little hateful animal which we have a mind to destroy. But my good star would have it, that he appeared pleased with my voice and gestures, and began to look upon me as a curiosity, much wondering to hear me pronounce articulate words, although he could not understand them. In the mean time I was not able to forbear groaning and shedding tears, and turning my head towards my sides; letting him know, as well as I could, how cruelly I was hurt by the pressure of his thumb and finger. He seemed to apprehend my meaning; for, lifting up the lappet of his coat, he put me gently into it, and immediately ran along with me to his master, who was a substantial farmer, and the same person I had first seen in the field.

The farmer, having (as I supposed by their talk) received

such an account of me as his servant could give him, took a piece of a small straw, about the size of a walking staff, and therewith lifted up the lappets of my coat; which it seems he thought to be some kind of covering that nature had given me. He blew my hairs aside to take a better view of my face. He called his hinds about him, and asked them (as I afterwards learned) whether they had ever seen in the fields any little creature that resembled me. He then placed me softly on the ground upon all four, but I got immediately up, and walked slowly backwards and forwards, to let those people see I had no intent to run away. They all sat down in a circle about me, the better to observe my motions. I pulled off my hat, and made a low bow towards the farmer. I fell on my knees, and lifted up my hands and eyes, and spoke several words as loud as I could : I took a purse of gold out of my pocket, and humbly presented it to him. He received it on the palm of his hand, then applied it close to his eye, to see what it was, and afterwards turned it several times with the point of a pin (which he took out of his sleeve), but could make nothing of it. Whereupon I made a sign that he should place his hand on the ground. I then took the purse, and opening it, poured all the gold into his palm. There were six Spanish pieces of four pistoles each, beside twenty or thirty smaller coins. I saw him wet the tip of his little finger upon his tongue, and take up one of my largest pieces, and then another, but he seemed wholly ignorant what they were. He made a sign to put them again into my purse, and the purse again into my pocket, which after offering to him several times, I thought it best to do.

The farmer by this time was convinced I must be a rational creature.

Gulliver's Travels, II, i

14

It is the custom that every Wednesday (which, as I have

before observed, was their Sabbath) the King and Queen, with the royal issue of both sexes, dine together in the apartment of his Majesty, to whom I was now become a favourite; and at these times my little chair and table were placed at his left hand before one of the salt-cellars. This prince took a pleasure in conversing with me, enquiring into the manners, religion, laws, government, and learning of Europe, wherein I gave him the best account I was able. His apprehension was so clear, and his judgment so exact, that he made very wise reflections and observations upon all I said. But I confess, that after I had been a little too copious in talking of my own beloved country, of our trade, and wars by sea and land, of our schisms in religion, and parties in the state, the prejudices of his education prevailed so far, that he could not forbear taking me up in his right hand, and stroking me gently with the other, after an hearty fit of laughing, asked me whether I were a Whig or a Tory. Then turning to his first minister, who waited behind him with a white staff, near as tall as the main-mast of the *Royal Sovereign*, he observed how con-temptible a thing was human grandeur, which could be mimicked by such diminutive insects as I: And yet, said he, I dare engage, those creatures have their titles and dis-tinctions of honour, they contrive little nests and burrows, that they call houses and cities; they make a figure in dress and equipage; they love, they fight, they dispute, they cheat, they betray. And thus he continued on, while my colour came and went several times with indignation to hear our noble country, the mistress of arts and arms, the scourge of France, the arbitress of Europe, the seat of virtue, piety, honour and truth, the pride and envy of the world, so contemptuously treated.

But, as I was not in a condition to resent injuries, so, upon mature thoughts, I began to doubt whether I were injured or no. For, after having been accustomed several months to the sight and converse of this people, and ob-served every object upon which I cast my eyes to be of

63

proportionable magnitude, the horror I had first conceived from their bulk and aspect was so far worn off, that if I had then beheld a company of English lords and ladies in their finery and birthday clothes, acting their several parts in the most courtly manner of strutting, and bowing, and prating, to say the truth, I should have been strongly tempted to laugh as much at them as this king and his grandees did at me. Neither indeed could I forbear smiling at my self, when the Queen used to place me upon her hand towards a looking-glass, by which both our persons appeared before me in full view together; and there could be nothing more ridiculous than the comparison : so that I really began to imagine myself dwindled many degrees below my usual size.

Gulliver's Travels, II, iii

15

His Majesty in another audience was at the pains to re-capitulate the sum of all I had spoken, compared the questions he made with the answers I had given; then taking me into his hands, and stroking me gently, delivered himself in these words, which I shall never forget, nor the manner he spoke them in : My little friend Grildrig, you have made a most admirable panegyric upon your country. You have clearly proved that ignorance, idleness and vice are the proper ingredients for qualifying a legislator. That laws are best explained, interpreted, and applied by those whose interest and abilities lie in perverting, confounding, and eluding them. I observe among you some lines of an institution, which in its original might have been tolerable, but these half erased, and the rest wholly blurred and blotted by corruptions. It doth not appear from all you have said, how any one perfection is required towards the procurement of any one station among you, much less that men are ennobled on account of their virtue, that priests are advanced for their piety or learning, soldiers for their conduct or valour, judges for their integrity, senators for the love of their country, or counsellors for their wisdom. As for yourself, continued the King, who have spent the greatest part of your life in travelling, I am well disposed to hope you may hitherto have escaped many vices of your country. But, by what I have gathered from your own relation, and the answers I have with much pains wringed and extorted from you, I cannot but conclude the bulk of your natives to be the most pernicious race of little odious vermin that nature ever suffered to crawl upon the surface of the earth.

Gulliver's Travels, II, vii

16

I have related the substance of several conversations I had with my master, during the greatest part of the time I had the honour to be in his service, but have indeed for brevity sake omitted much more than is here set down.

When I had answered all his questions, and his curiosity, seemed to be fully satisfied, he sent for me one morning early, and commanding me to sit down at some distance (an honour which he had never before conferred upon me), he said he had been very seriously considering my whole story, as far as it related both to myself and my country : that he looked upon us as a sort of animals to whose share, by what accident he could not conjecture, some small pittance of reason had fallen, whereof we made no other use than by its assistance to aggravate our natural corruptions, and to acquire new ones which Nature had not given us. That we disarmed ourselves of the few abilities she had bestowed, had been very successful in multiplying our original wants, and seemed to spend our whole lives in vain endeavours to supply them by our own inventions. That as to myself, it was manifest I had neither the strength or agility of a common yahoo, that I walked infirmly on my hinder feet, had found out a contrivance to make my claws of no use or defence, and to remove the hair from my chin, which was intended as a shelter from the sun and the weather. Lastly, that I could neither run with speed, nor climb trees like my brethren (as he called them) the yahoos in this country.

That our institutions of government and law were plainly owing to our gross defects in reason, and by consequence, in virtue; because reason alone is sufficient to govern a rational creature; which was therefore a character we had no pretence to challenge, even from the account I had given of my own people, although he manifestly perceived that in order to favour them I had concealed many particulars, and often *said the thing which was not*.

He was the more confirmed in this opinion, because he observed, that as I agreed in every feature of my body with other yahoos, except where it was to my real disadvantage in point of strength, speed, and activity, the shortness of my claws, and some other particulars where nature had no part; so from the representation I had given him of our lives, our manners, and our actions, he found as near a resemblance in the disposition of our minds. He said the yahoos were known to hate one another more than they did any different species of animals; and the reason usually assigned was the odiousness of their own shapes, which all could see in the rest, but not in themselves. He had therefore begun to think it not unwise in us to cover our bodies, and, by that invention, and, by that invention, conceal many of our deformities from each other, which would else be hardly supportable. But he now found he had been mistaken, and that the dissensions of those brutes in his country were owing to the same cause with ours, as I had described them. For if (said he) you throw among five yahoos as much food as would be sufficient for fifty, they will, instead of eating peaceably, fall together by the ears, each single one impatient to have all to itself, and therefore a servant was usually employed to stand by while they were feeding abroad, and those kept at home were tied at a distance from each other; that if a cow died of age or accident, before a Houyhnhnm could secure it for his own yahoos, those in the neighbourhood would come in herds to seize it, and then would ensue such a battle as I had described, with terrible wounds made by their claws on both sides, although they seldom were able to kill one another, for want of such convenient instruments of death as we had invented. At other times the like battles have been fought between the yahoos of several neighbourhoods without any visible cause; those of one district watching all opportunities to surprise the next before they are prepared. But if they find their project hath miscarried, they return home, and, for want of enemies, engage in what I call a civil war among themselves.

That in some fields of his country there are certain shining stones of several colours, whereof the yahoos are violently fond, and when part of these stones are fixed in the earth, as it sometimes happeneth, they will dig with their claws for whole days to get them out, carry them away, and hide them by heaps in their kennels; but still looking round with great caution, for fear their comrades should find out their treasure. My master said, he could never discover the reason of this unnatural appetite, or how these stones could be of any use to a yahoo; but now he believed it might proceed from the same principle of avarice which I had ascribed to mankind; that he had once, by way of experiment, privately removed a heap of these stones from the place where one of his yahoos had buried it : whereupon the sordid animal, missing his treasure, by his loud lamenting brought the whole herd to the place, there miserably howled, then fell to biting and tearing the rest, began to pine away, would neither eat, nor sleep, nor work, till he ordered a servant privately to convey the stones into the same hole and hide them as before; which when his yahoo had found, he presently recovered his spirits and good humour, but took care to remove them to a better hiding-place, and hath ever since been a very serviceable brute.

My master farther assured me, which I also observed myself, that in the fields where these shining stones abound, the fiercest and most frequent battles are fought, occasioned by perpetual inroads of the neighbouring yahoos.

He said, it was common, when two yahoos discovered such a stone in a field, and were contending which of them should be the proprietor, a third would take the advantage, and carry it away from them both; which my master would needs contend to have some resemblance with our suits at law; wherein I thought it for our credit not to undeceive him; since the decision he mentioned was much more equitable than many decrees among us : because the plaintiff and defendant there lost nothing beside the stone they contended for, whereas our courts of equity would never have dismissed the cause while either of them had any thing left.

Gulliver's Travels, IV, vii

A dominant image in *Gulliver's Travels* is that of the animal, and its relation to man. An ancient definition of man, surviving in Swift's day, was 'animal rationale', a rational animal, an animal which possesses reason; one way of describing the *Travels* (though like any short description it is very inadequate to the work as a whole) would be to say that it is an investigation of human character, actions, institutions, and beliefs in relation to that definition. *Is* man a rational animal, Swift makes us ask, and if so quite what does the definition imply about ourselves? In what sense are we animals? In what sense rational?

In the different voyages, man's animality and rationality are looked at in different ways, mounting to a climax in the *Voyage to the Houyhnhnms*. The first extract above is from Gulliver's Voyage to Lilliput, whose inhabitants are about six inches high. Gulliver first sees them swarming over him, having captured him in his sleep, and this sense of them as little animals, clever pets like trained mice, never quite leaves him although they are an intelligent little people. The perspective in which Gulliver sees human nature in the shape of 'a human creature not six inches high' enables the reader himself to see more clearly the relation of human reason to human passions and instincts (the animal). Gulliver treats the Lilliputians kindly, but when he leaves he reveals how readily he still thinks of them—because they are smaller than the humans he is used to—as not so different from animals. As he is taking the tiny cattle home, 'to propagate the breed', so he would have taken 'a dozen of the natives', without considering them as individual humans, who might be distressed at being so treated.

The implications of this incident are developed in the second extract. Gulliver, landing in the country of the giants, sees one coming towards him, and realises that he is now in the position of a Lilliputian. The animal imagery here is much more explicit; the giant is half-afraid of Gulliver, as of 'a small dangerous animal' like a weasel. He has never seen 'any little creature' like Gulliver, and can make nothing of him; he does not recognise him as a small human being and Gulliver has to work hard to show that he is 'a rational creature'. The first impression he makes is of an animal.

The third extract is also from the second voyage; a further dimension is added to the animal comparison through the moral perceptiveness of the good king of the giants. The king draws from the animal comparison the very conclusion that the reader is intended to draw : 'how contemptible a thing was human grandeur, which could be mimicked by such diminutive insects as I'. The tiny

Gulliver, so self-important about the great affairs of his diminutive country, is absurd to the huge king; he is an insect. But the king is wise enough to see that in that case, larger men like himself are only larger insects, who make nests and burrows as the animals do, and whose animal passions compel them, in contradiction to their reason, to cheat and betray. In the fourth extract, the giant king is so horrified by Gulliver's account of his race that what had seemed to the kindly giant rather charming and pathetic 'diminutive insects' become instead a 'race of little odious vermin'.

The last extract is from the fourth voyage, where the imagery of man the animal is extended and centralised in the Yahoos, symbol of the animal part of the nature of man (but not *identical* with man, since human nature also includes reason, which Yahoo nature does not). The Houyhnhnms, creatures entirely governed by reason (and so also differing from man) can, however, see little difference between Gulliver and the Yahoos. Gulliver's master Houyhnhnm here gives him an account of the conclusions he has come to. He sees men not precisely as rational animals (which is what he himself is) but as 'a sort of animals to whose share . . . some small pittance of reason had fallen'. He gives a detailed account of the way men and Yahoos resemble each other (the Yahoo instincts are all primitive animal versions of human vices of avarice, destructiveness, etc.) and concludes that men have made use of their pittance of reason not to control but to aggravate their natural corruptions: the animal in man too often outweighs the rational. The repulsive details of the description of the Yahoos take the animal imagery of the *Travels* to its meaningful climax.

Swift's use of imagery is flexible, and one must not

assume that the comparison of men with animals, for instance, has the same meaning and serves the same purpose everywhere in his work. It is used in different ways according to the satiric meaning he wants to express. In the extracts from *Gulliver's Travels*, the animal comparison serves subtly different purposes in each book, and these differences should be observed.

In *A Modest Proposal* Swift's purpose is much more specific than in *Gulliver's Travels*. He is fighting a particular set of circumstances in contemporary Ireland, and he is concerned to show that the policy of the English government, the irresponsibility and cupidity of the landlords, and the despondency and moral degeneracy of many of the poor inhabitants, dispirited by the hopelessness of their situation, have made the poor behave like animals. If men are treated like beasts, the imagery implies, they will come to act like beasts. More precisely still, Swift believed that many of the ills of Ireland were caused by the wholesale conversion of arable land to pasture; the keeping of sheep was more immediately profitable to the owners of country estates, and sheep-farming required fewer labourers, so that many were thrown out of work. Thus one could for satiric purpose put it that, to judge by events, cattle are thought more important than people in Ireland; and that calves and lambs, well fed during their brief lives, are happier and better looked after than the children of the poor. Lambs are profitable to their owners; children are a financial burden. Perhaps if children could be made, by a scheme like the one set out in *A Modest Proposal*, as profitable as beasts, they would be more humanely treated. So the comparison of man to beast is developed with precision in the following extract.

Fifthly, this food would likewise bring great custom to taverns, where the vintners will certainly be so prudent as to procure the best receipts for dressing it to perfection, and consequently have their houses frequented by all the fine gentlemen, who justly value themselves upon their knowledge in good eating; and a skilful cook, who understands how to oblige his guests, will contrive to make it as expensive as they please.

Sixthly, this would be a great inducement to marriage, which all wise nations have either encouraged by rewards, or enforced by laws and penalties. It would increase the care and tenderness of mothers towards their children, when they were sure of a settlement for life, to the poor babes, provided in some sort by the public to their annual profit instead of expense. We should soon see an honest emulation among the married women, which of them could bring the fattest child to the market. Men would become as fond of their wives, during the time of pregnancy, as they are now of their mares in foal, their cows in calf, or sows when they are ready to farrow, nor offer to beat or kick them (as it is too frequent a practice) for fear of a miscarriage.

Many other advantages might be enumerated. For instance, the addition of some thousand carcasses in our exportation of barrelled beef; the propagation of swine's flesh, and improvement in the art of making good bacon, so much wanted among us by the great destruction of pigs, too frequent at our tables, are no way comparable in taste of magnificence to a well-grown, fat yearling child, which roasted whole will make a considerable figure at a Lord Mayor's feast, or any other public entertainment. But this and many others I omit, being studious of brevity.

Supposing that one thousand families in this city would be constant customers for infants flesh, besides others who might have it at merry meetings, particularly weddings and christenings; I compute that Dublin would take off annually about twenty thousand carcasses, and the rest of the kingdom (where probably they will be sold somewhat cheaper) the remaining eighty thousand.

A Modest Proposal, etc.

Examine the dispassionate language in which the persona discusses the advantages his proposal will produce. He uses, to apply to the children, words and phrases normally associated only with slaughtered animals: 'dressing it' (for serving at table), 'carcasses', 'yearling child', 'roasted whole'. Similarly there is a parallel, calmly assumed by the persona, between women in pregnancy and 'mares in foal', 'cows in calf'. What does this vocabulary suggest about (a) the situation of the Irish poor—is it one that is likely to make them behave humanely? (b) the mentality of the proposer, and of those economists of the time who brought forward schemes to prevent people being a financial burden to their country?

Look for similar imagery in the earlier extract from *A Modest Proposal* (Extract 11), and identify precisely the satiric effect of each occurrence, e.g., such terms as 'breeders', 'the fore or hind quarter', 'excellent nutritive meat'.

Use of contemporary attitudes, ideas and institutions for satiric purpose

The Battle of the Books, like *A Tale of A Tub*, with which it was published, was written in the 1690s, and is a contribution to the 'Quarrel of the Ancients and the Moderns', which engaged many philosophers, scientists, and literary men in seventeenth century England and France. The matter at issue in the 'Quarrel' was whether the achievements of modern nations could be compared to those of the ancient classical nations of Rome and Greece; and though it at first seems to us a trivial argument, implicit in it was an issue of genuine importance: is modern man justified in developing his own ideas, inventions, and ways of writing, or is he fit only to work within the traditions handed down from classical philosophers, scientists, and men of letters through centuries of a Christianised classicism? Is man, with the universe he lives in, slowly deteriorating, as many supposed, or are they essentially unchanged? For if man is not now inferior to his ancestors he, with the added knowledge of the centuries, may even surpass the ancients.

In England the seventeenth century was the great age of the development of experimental science, and to the new scientists it was especially necessary to feel free of the traditional views of thinkers like Aristotle. But the argument also involved philosophy, practical inventions (like printing and gunpowder, on which moderns prided themselves), scholarship, and literature, all opening up new ways in the seventeenth and eighteenth centuries. Swift includes in the *Battle* original modern thinkers like Bacon and Descartes, and mentions improvements of which the moderns were proud (in architecture, the art of fortification, and mathematics). But the chief concern in the *Battle* is literary and scholarly, for Swift wrote it in support of his patron and friend Sir William Temple, who had rashly taken part in the debate on the side of the ancients and had given, as examples of ancient achievement, certain literary works which his opponents (William Wotton and the great Greek textual scholar Richard Bentley) showed to be spurious. Swift therefore attempts to ridicule the whole 'modern' position, through an allegory in which the ancient and modern books in St. James's Library, the Royal Library in which Bentley was librarian, fight a battle. The allegory ingeniously points, not to the textual rights and wrongs of the Temple-Bentley dispute, but to those qualities in the supporters of modern supremacy which Swift found so objectionable as to discredit their case.

18

Things were at this crisis, when a material accident fell out. For, upon the highest corner of a large window, there dwelt a certain spider, swollen up to the first magnitude by the destruction of infinite numbers of flies, whose spoils lay scattered before the gates of his palace, like human bones before the cave of some giant. The avenues to his castle were guarded with turnpikes and palisadoes, all after the modern way of fortification. After you had passed several courts, you came to the center, wherein you might behold the constable himself in his own lodgings, which had windows fronting to each avenue, and ports to sally out upon all occasions of prey or defence. In this mansion he had for some time dwelt in peace and plenty, without danger to his person by swallows from above, or to his palace by brooms from below, when it was the pleasure of fortune to conduct thither a wandering bee, to whose curiosity a broken pane in the glass had discovered itself, and in he went; where expatiating a while, he at last happened to alight upon one of the outward walls of the spider's citadel; which, yielding to the unequal weight, sunk down to the very foundation. Thrice he endeavoured to force his passage, and thrice the center shook. The spider within, feeling the terrible convulsion, supposed at first that nature was approaching to her final dissolution; or else that Beelzebub, with all his legions, was come to revenge the death of many thousands of his subjects, whom his enemy had slain and devoured. However, he at length valiantly resolved to issue forth, and meet his fate. Meanwhile the bee had acquainted himself of his toils, and posted securely at some distance, was employed in cleansing his wings, and disengaging them from the ragged remnants of the cobweb. By this time the spider was adventured out, when beholding the chasms, and ruins, and dilapidations of his fortress, he was very near at his wit's end; he stormed and swore like a madman, and swelled till he was ready to burst. At length, casting his eye upon the bee, and wisely gathering causes from events (for they knew each other by sight), 'A plague split you,' said he, 'for a giddy son of a whore. Is it you, with a vengeance, that have made this litter here? Could you not look before you, and be d—nd? Do you think I have nothing else to do (in the devil's name) but to mend and repair after your arse?' 'Good words, friend,' said the bee (having now pruned himself, and being disposed to droll) 'I'll give you my hand and word to come near your kennel no more; I was never in such a confounded pickle since I was born.' 'Sirrah,' replied the spider, 'if it were not for breaking an old custom in our family, never to stir abroad against an enemy, I should come and teach you better manners.' 'I pray have patience,' said the bee, 'or you will spend your substance, and for aught I see, you may stand in need of it all, towards the repair of your house.' 'Rogue, rogue,' replied the spider, 'yet methinks you should have more respect to a person, whom all the world allows to be so much your betters.' 'By my troth,' said the bee, 'the comparison will amount to a very good jest, and you will do me a favour to let me know the reasons that all the world is pleased to use in so hopeful a dispute.' At this the spider, having swelled himself into the size and posture of a disputant, began his argument in the true spirit of controversy, with a resolution to be heartily scurrilous and angry, to urge on his own reasons, without the least regard to the answers or objections of his opposite, and fully predetermined in his mind against all conviction.

'Not to disparage myself,' said he, 'by the comparison with such a rascal, what art thou but a vagabond without house or home, without stock or inheritance, born to no possession of your own, but a pair of wings and a drone-pipe? Your livelihood is an universal plunder upon nature; a freebooter over fields and gardens; and for the sake of stealing will rob a nettle as easily as a violet. Whereas I am a domestic animal, furnished with a native stock within myself. This large castle (to show my improvements in the mathematics) is all built with my own hands, and the materials extracted altogether out of my own person.'

'I am glad,' answered the bee, 'to hear you grant at least that I am come honestly by my wings and my voice; for then, it seems, I am obliged to Heaven alone for my flights and my music; and Providence would never have bestowed on me two such gifts, without designing them for the noblest ends. I visit indeed all the flowers and blossoms of the field and the garden; but whatever I collect from thence enriches myself, without the least injury to their beauty, their smell, or their taste. Now, for you and your skill in architecture and other mathematics, I have little to say: in that building of yours there might, for aught I know, have been labor and method enough, but by woful experience for us both, 'tis too plain, the materials are naught, and I hope you will henceforth take warning, and consider duration and matter as well as method and art. You boast, indeed, of being obliged to no other creature, but of drawing and spinning out all from yourself; that is to say, if we may judge of the liquor in the vessel by what issues out, you possess a good plentiful store of dirt and poison in your breast; and, tho' I would by no means lessen or disparage your genuine stock of either, yet I doubt you are somewhat obliged for an increase of both, to a little foreign assistance. Your inherent portion of dirt does not fail of acquisitions, by sweepings exhaled from below; and one insect furnishes you with a share of poison to destroy another. So that in short, the question comes all to this—which is the nobler being of the two, that which by a lazy contemplation of four inches round, by an overweening pride, feeding and engendering on itself, turns all into excrement and venom, produces nothing at last, but flybane and a cobweb; or that which, by an universal range, with long search, much study, true judgment, and distinction of things, brings home honey and wax.'

This dispute was managed with such eagerness, clamor, and warmth, that the two parties of books in arms below stood silent a while, waiting in suspense what would be the issue, which was not long undetermined, for the bee grown impatient at so much loss of time, fled straight away to a bed of roses, without looking for a reply, and left the spider like an orator, collected in himself and just prepared to burst out.

It happened upon this emergency, the Æsop broke silence first. . . . 'The disputants,' said he, 'have admirably managed the dispute between them, have taken in the full strength of all that is to be said on both sides, and exhausted the substance of every argument *pro* and *con*. It is but to adjust the reasonings of both to the present quarrel, then to compare and apply the labors and fruits of each as the bee has learnedly deduced them; and we shall find the conclusions fall plain and close upon the Moderns and us. For pray gentlemen, was ever anything so modern as the spider in his air, his turns, and his paradoxes? He argues in the behalf of you his brethren and himself, with many boastings of his native stock and great genius, that he spins and spits wholly from himself, and scorns to own any obligation or assistance from without. Then he displays to you his great skill in architecture, and improvement in the mathematics. To all this the bee, as an advocate retained by us the Ancients, thinks fit to answer; that if one may judge of the great genius or inventions of the Moderns by what they have produced, you will hardly have countenance to bear you out in boasting of either. Erect your schemes with as much method and skill as you please; yet if the materials be nothing but dirt, spun out of your own entrails (the guts of modern brains) the edifice will conclude at last in a cobweb, the duration of which, like that of other spiders' webs, may be imputed to their being forgotten, or neglected, or hid in a corner. For anything else of genuine that the Moderns may pretend to, I cannot recollect, unless it be a large vein of wrangling and satire, much of a nature and substance with the spider's poison; which, however, they pretend to spit wholly out of themselves, is improved by the same arts, by feeding upon the insects and vermin of the age. As for us the Ancients, we are content with the bee to pretend to nothing of our own, beyond our wings and our voice, that is to say, our flights and our language. For the rest, whatever we have got, has been by infinite labor and search, and ranging through every corner of nature; the difference is, that instead of dirt and poison, we have rather chose to fill our hives with honey and wax, thus furnishing mankind with the two noblest of things, which are sweetness and light.'

The Battle of the Books

Into a pause in the battle between the two armies of books, Swift sets a further allegorical incident, the encounter between the bee and the spider whose web is spun in a corner of the library. This presents more explicitly what was, for him, the real issue: not whether this or that modern book is as good as this or that ancient one (although, indeed, his ancients for the most part come off best in the battle) but whether the modern attitudes, and the books which embody them, make men better, wiser, and more truly civilised than do those which had been handed down from the ancient world and had long been a part of the civilisation and education of Europe. According to this criterion (itself based on the traditional view of humanist thought that literature ought to make its readers better and wiser) Swift finds that the moderns are inferior.

Thus in the extract above the spider stands for the moderns, and his barbarous and crude way of talking (which refers partly to Bentley's overbearing controversial manner), his blustering arrogance, conceit, and over-valuing of his flimsy achievement—the cobweb which in his opinion is a solidly built fortress—express Swift's view of the qualities which independent modernity, and a disregard for traditional values, must encourage. The spider is chosen as the image of the moderns not only for its generally unpleasing nature but for more specific reasons: it spins everything out of its own entrails, as the moderns insist on the importance of their own ideas and pay no attention to the wisdom learned over the centuries, and as a result it produces only a flimsy and dusty cobweb for all its self-conceit: also it is poisonous (virulent in controversy). The bee, on the other hand, follows ancient tradition, and produces the honey and wax which provide us with 'sweetness and light'—delight and wisdom. It creates not out of its own entrails, or individual ideas, but out of flowers, the world of things outside itself, and is guided by earlier creators. Aesop, the writer of moral beast fables, appropriately makes the application.

The individualistic and self-deceived modern spider has much in common with the persona of *A Tale of a Tub*. A comparison of the two helps to clarify the nature of Swift's satiric target in each case. Compare particularly Extract 20, to which Swift appends a note about 'metaphysical cobweb problems'.

Discuss Swift's view of the right and wrong kinds of originality in thinking and writing (as seen in the bee and the spider respectively, and in Aesop's comments). Is this view compatible with our own twentieth-century ideas of what constitutes 'original' thinking and writing?

Gulliver's third voyage takes him first to Laputa, an island floating above the earth and inhabited by men who devote themselves so exclusively to the abstract sciences of mathematics, astronomy, and music that they are unaware of what goes on around them. These impractical people embody Swift's amusement at those of his contemporaries who—to his mind—neglect the realities of a moral and practical life to engage in abstruse speculation. Like so many objects of his satire, they have alienated themselves from reality.

The importance of mathematics to the study of science (especially astronomy) and philosophy was being stressed at this time, and the three sciences on which the Laputans concentrate are traditionally the most abstract of all. Swift uses them, accordingly, to suggest the readiness with which man turns from what should concern him, a virtuous, peaceful, and if possible comfortable life, to studies of less value to him. The 'airy region' Laputa is a flying island to symbolise the people's lack of 'down-to-earth' qualities.

In this extract Gulliver is in Balnibarbi, the fixed land over which Laputa hovers and which it rules.

19

I had hitherto seen only one side of the Academy, the other being appropriated to the advancers of speculative learning, of whom I shall say something when I have mentioned one illustrious person more, who is called among them 'the universal artist'. He told us he had been thirty years employing his thoughts for the improvement of human life. He had two large rooms full of wonderful curiosities, and fifty men at work. Some were condensing air into a dry tangible substance, by extracting the nitre, and letting the aqueous or fluid particles percolate; others softening marble for pillows and pincushions; others petrifying the hoofs of a living horse to preserve them from foundering. The artist himself was at that time busy upon two great designs; the first, to sow land with chaff, wherein he affirmed the true seminal virtue to be contained, as he demonstrated by several experiments which I was not skilful enough to comprehend. The other was, by a certain composition of gums, minerals, and vegetables outwardly applied to prevent the growth of wool upon two young lambs; and he hoped in a reasonable time to propagate the breed of naked sheep all over the kingdom.

We crossed a walk to the other part of the Academy, where, as I have already said, the projectors in speculative learning resided.

The first professor I saw was in a very large room, with forty pupils about him. After salutation, observing me to look earnestly upon a frame, which took up the greatest part of both the length and breadth of the room, he said perhaps I might wonder to see him employed in a project for improving speculative knowledge by practical and mechanical operations. But the world would soon be sensible of its usefulness, and he flattered himself that a more noble, exalted thought never sprang in any other man's head. Every one knows how laborious the usual method is of attaining to arts and sciences; whereas by his contrivance the most ignorant person at a reasonable charge, and with a little bodily labour, may write books in philosophy, poetry, politics, law, mathematics and theology, without the least assistance from genius or study. He then led me to the frame, about the sides whereof all his pupils stood in ranks. It was twenty foot square, placed in the middle of the room. The superficies was composed of several bits of wood, about the bigness of a die, but some larger than others. They were all linked together by slender wires. These bits of wood were covered on every square with papers pasted on them, and on these papers were written all the words of their language in their several moods, tenses, and declensions, but without any order. The professor then desired me to observe, for he was going to set his engine at work. The pupils at his command took each of them hold of an iron handle, whereof there were forty fixed round the edges of the frame, and giving them a sudden turn, the whole disposition of the words was entirely changed. He then commanded six and thirty of the lads to read the several lines softly as they appeared upon the frame; and where they found three or four words together that might make part of a sentence, they dictated to the four remaining boys who were scribes. This work was repeated three or four times, and at every turn the engine was so contrived, that the words shifted into new places, as the square bits of wood moved upside down.

Six hours a day the young students were employed in this labour, and the professor showed me several volumes in large folio already collected, of broken sentences, which he intended to piece together, and out of those rich materials to give the world a complete body of all arts and sciences; which however might be still improved, and much expedited, if the public would raise a fund for making and employing five hundred such frames in Lagado, and oblige the managers to contribute in common their several collections.

He assured me, that this invention had employed all his thoughts from his youth, that he had emptied the whole vocabulary into his frame, and made the strictest computation of the general proportion there is in books between the numbers of particles, nouns, and verbs, and other parts of speech.

I made my humblest acknowledgements to this illustrious person for his great communicativeness, and promised if ever I had the good fortune to return to my native country, that I would do him justice, as the sole inventor of this wonderful machine; the form and contrivance of which I desired leave to delineate upon paper as in the figure here annexed. I told him, although it were the custom of our learned in Europe to steal inventions from each other, who had thereby at least this advantage, that it became a controversy which was the right owner, yet I would take such caution, that he should have the honour entire without a rival.

We next went to the school of languages, where three professors sat in consultation upon improving that of their own country.

The first project was to shorten discourse by cutting poly-syllables into one, and leaving out verbs and participles, because in reality all things imaginable are but nouns.

The other was a scheme for entirely abolishing all words whatsoever; and this was urged as a great advantage in point of health as well as brevity. For it is plain, that every word we speak is in some degree a diminution of our lungs by corrosion, and consequently contributes to the shortening of our lives. An expedient was therefore offered, that since words are only names for *things*, it would be more convenient for all men to carry about them such *things* as were necessary to express the particular business they are to discourse on. And this invention would certainly have taken place, to the great ease as well as health of the subject, if the women in conjunction with the vulgar and illiterate had not threatened to raise a rebellion, unless they might be allowed the liberty to speak with their tongues, after the manner of their forefathers; such constant irreconcilable enemies to science are the common people. However, many of the most learned and wise adhere to the new scheme of expressing themselves by *things*, which hath only this inconvenience attending it, that if a man's business be very great, and of various kinds, he must be obliged in proportion to carry a greater bundle of *things* upon his back, unless he can afford one or two strong servants to attend him. I have often beheld two of those sages almost sinking under the weight of their packs, like pedlars among us; who when they met in the streets would lay down their loads, open their sacks and hold conversation for an hour together; then put up their implements, help each other to resume their burthens, and take their leave.

But for short conversations a man may carry implements in his pockets and under his arms, enough to supply him, and in his house he cannot be at a loss; therefore the room where company meet who practise this art is full of all *things* ready at hand, requisite to furnish matter for this kind of artificial converse.

Gulliver's Travels, III, v

Once a flourishing country, Balnibarbi has been ruined by the spread of unrealistic ideas from Laputa. An 'Academy of Projectors' has been set up, Swift's satiric version of that distinguished body of early experimental scientists, the recently founded Royal Society. Some of the many experiments described were based on actual experiments of the Society, though exaggerated. The activities of the 'universal artist' are in themselves a neat allegorical summary of what Swift is attacking through his Academy. The artist's experiments are ingenious but wrong-headed; for, far from contributing to useful knowledge, they turn the already useful into the useless and pointless. Thus the usefulness of marble is that it is hard, and of sheep that they bear wool, but the artist is busy at softening marble and breeding naked sheep. The fact that the Royal Society did of necessity undertake investigations which seemed, in the short run, pointless, made the Academy a handy equivalent to the habit of mind Swift is ridiculing.

The 'universal artist' supposes he can encompass all knowledge. His colleague the professor is providing a machine by which this can be done without either genius or study. He is akin to the persona of the *Tale*, who has ways of becoming 'learned' and impressive without reading a book. Swift is pointing to the superficial learning of 'modern' authors. The persona of the *Tale*, the artist, and the professor achieve knowledge, Swift suggests, only as a machine might achieve it; the profound and difficult thought of great writers exists, in the minds of such trivial and superficial men, only as a random collection of phrases. The proposal to substitute 'things' for 'words' is Swift's way of laughing at scientifically-minded members of the Royal Society who wished to make language less metaphorical and imaginative, and more factually precise, like the language proper to reporting experiments. Each 'name' should correspond to one 'thing', and the name should be expressive of the thing's nature. Swift, with his writer's feeling for language as a rich living thing developed unscientifically over the centuries, sees such plans as ridiculous and stultifying. The language resulting would be as clumsy and inexpressive as if one carried 'things' about to communicate by, and as dead as the universal artist's living horse with petrified hoofs. The 'new science' thus becomes a symbol of all kinds of useless, superficial, mechanical, and irrelevant mental activity which keeps us away from useful thinking.

The following passage is part of the most complicated piece of irony in the *Tale*, the 'Digression Concerning Madness', in which the persona praises 'madness' (a conceited personal individuality which leads to a lack of proportion and to delusion) as the source of many blessings of mankind. Those who introduce new religions and philosophies, and those who are great conquerors, are all in this sense mad. The Digression is the climax of a work in which Swift has shown, through the allegory of the churches and through the foolish opinions of the persona, how much confusion is produced by such 'madness', an insistence that *one's own* opinions and interests are superior to other peoples', and an insistence that other people accept them. Such an illusion of one's own self-importance and of one's own special ability to know the truth makes one a dangerous nuisance to others, and Swift sees it as especially a modern vice though he recognises its existence in all ages.

20

There is in mankind a certain   *   *   *   *   *
*   *   *   *   *   *   *   *   *   *   *
    Hic multa   *   *   *   *   *   *   *   *
desiderantur   *   *   *   *   *   *   *   *
*   *   *   And this I take to be a clear solution of the matter.

Having therefore so narrowly passed through this intricate difficulty, the reader will, I am sure, agree with me in the conclusion, that if the moderns mean by madness, only a disturbance or transposition of the brain, by force of certain vapours issuing up from the lower faculties, then has this madness been the parent of all those mighty revolutions that have happened in empire, in philosophy, and in religion. For the brain in its natural position and state of serenity, disposeth its owner to pass his life in the common forms, without any thought of subduing multitudes to his own power, his reasons, or his visions; and the more he shapes his understanding by the pattern of human learning, the less he is inclined to form parties after his particular notions, because that instructs him in his private infirmities, as well as in the stubborn ignorance of the people. But when a man's fancy gets astride on his reason, when imagination is at cuffs with the senses, and common understanding, as well as common sense, is kicked out of doors, the first proselyte he makes is himself; and when that is once compassed, the difficulty is not so great in bringing over others; a strong delusion always operating from without as vigorously as from within. For, cant and vision are to the ear and the eye, the same that tickling is to the touch. Those entertainments and pleasures we most value in life, are such as dupe and play the wag with the senses. For, if we take an examination of what is generally understood by happiness, as it has respect either to the understanding or the senses, we shall find all its properties and adjuncts will herd under this short definition, that it is a perpetual possession of being well deceived. And first, with relation to the mind or understanding, 'tis manifest what mighty advantages fiction has over truth; and the reason is just at our elbow, because imagination can build nobler scenes, and produce more wonderful revolutions than fortune or nature will be at expense to furnish. Nor is mankind so much to blame in his choice thus determining him, if we consider that the debate merely lies between things past and things conceived; and so the question is only this—

88

whether things that have place in the imagination, may not as properly be said to exist, as those that are seated in the memory, which may be justly held in the affirmative, and very much to the advantage of the former, since this is acknowledged to be the womb of things, and the other allowed to be no more than the grave. Again, if we take this definition of happiness, and examine it with reference to the senses, it will be acknowledged wonderfully adapt. How fading and insipid do all objects accost us, that are not conveyed in the vehicle of delusion? How shrunk is everything, as it appears in the glass of nature? So that if it were not for the assistance of artificial mediums, false lights, refracted angles, varnish, and tinsel, there would be a mighty level in the felicity and enjoyments of mortal men. If this were seriously considered by the world, as I have a certain reason to suspect it hardly will, men would no longer reckon among their high points of wisdom, the art of exposing weak sides, and publishing infirmities; an employment, in my opinion, neither better nor worse than that of unmasking, which I think has never been allowed fair usage, either in the world or the play-house.

In the proportion that credulity is a more peaceful possession of the mind than curiosity; so far preferable is that wisdom, which converses about the surface, to that pretended philosophy which enters into the depth of things, and then comes gravely back with informations and discoveries, that in the inside they are good for nothing. The two senses, to which all objects first address themselves, are the sight and the touch; these never examine farther than the colour, the shape, the size, and whatever other qualities dwell, or are drawn by art upon the outward of bodies; and then comes reason officiously with tools for cutting, and opening, and mangling, and piercing, offering to demonstrate, that they are not of the same consistence quite through. Now, I take all this to be the last degree of perverting nature; one of whose eternal laws it is, to put her best furniture forward. And therefore, in order to save the charges of all such expensive anatomy for the time to come, I do here think fit to inform the reader, that in such conclusions as these, reason is certainly in the right, and that in most corporeal beings, which have fallen under my cognizance, the outside hath been infinitely preferable to the in; whereof I have been farther convinced from some late experiments. Last week I saw a woman flayed, and you will hardly believe how much it altered her person for the worse. Yesterday I ordered the carcass of a beau to be stripped in my presence, when we were all amazed to find so many unsuspected faults under one suit of clothes. Then I laid open his brain, his heart, and his spleen; but I plainly perceived at every operation, that the farther we proceeded, we found the defects increase upon us in number and bulk; from all which, I justly formed this conclusion to myself; that whatever philosopher or projector can find out an art to sodder and patch up the flaws and imperfections of nature, will deserve much better of mankind, and teach us a more useful science, than that so much in present esteem, of widening and exposing them (like him who held anatomy to be the ultimate end of physic). And he, whose fortunes and dispositions have placed him in a convenient station to enjoy the fruits of this noble art; he that can with Epicurus content his ideas with the films and images that fly off upon his senses from the superficies of things; such a man truly wise, creams off nature, leaving the sour and the dregs for philosophy and reason to lap up. This is the sublime and refined point of felicity, called, the possession of being well deceived; the serene peaceful state of being a fool among knaves.

A Tale of a Tub, Section IX:
'A Digression Concerning Madness'

'Madness' in the *Tale* is, then, an extreme form of that state, of conceited self-deception and alienation from reality, to which all human beings are prone to a lesser degree. To present it, Swift causes his persona to use certain concepts familiar to his contemporaries. The boasted originality of the mad is due merely to physical causes (compare the eccentric Aeolists in Extract 21), and for those causes Swift draws upon seventeenth-century medical theory. The persona's insistence that the evidence of the senses, rather than that of the reason, should be followed, is a reference to the philosophy of Epicurus, well-known at that time; but its implications are fully appreciated when one remembers that the philosophers and scientists of Swift's time often had occasion to discuss the question. The new instruments, microscope and telescope, showed how unreliable man's senses were as a guide to reality, for now tiny creatures and huge celestial bodies became visible for the first time. The persona is deliberately refusing to face such evidence because it is more pleasant to rely on the senses than to follow the often uncomfortable conclusions of rational thought. Better to be credulous, he says, than to look too deeply into things. To reason is to spoil things, to analyse is to destroy. The examples he brings to prove this (flaying a woman, dissecting a fashionable beau) reveal his inability to know what the processes of reason are. Reason is not, to him, a constructive and corrective process, which brings one nearer to a knowledge of reality; it is a destructive one, for it destroys pleasing illusions. The credulous, the deliberately deceived, may be fools, but the reasoners are knaves; he prefers to be a fool. The pretended 'defect in the manuscript', with which the extract opens, is itself a comment on the persona's pretension, incapacity to think, and preference for the easy way. Swift's note remarks: 'Here is another defect in the manuscript, but I think the author did wisely, and that the matter which

91

thus strained his faculties, was not worth a solution; and it were well if all metaphysical cobweb problems were no otherwise answered.'

Examine the ways in which Swift discredits his author's argument (e.g., the use of such words as 'varnish' and 'tinsel', 'films' and 'images', and the definition of felicity at the close).

The Aeolists are a religious sect of Swift's own invention, but their beliefs and practices are so conceived as to satirise those of various nonconformist, or dissenting, sects as they appeared to the Anglicans. Dissenters were often ridiculed for the claim made by some of the sects to a divine inspiration which issued in ecstasies and in emotionally excitable sermons and prayers. In the Aeolists Swift satirises false claims to inspiration; what they take to be spiritual ecstasy is in fact due to mere physical excitement which has confused their wits. The description of the Aeolists' distorted mouths and protruding eyes is aimed at the grimaces and the nasal tone which were said to accompany inspirational preaching. The Dissenters' claim was seen by those of Swift's persuasion as a self-deluded arrogance of the same kind as that of the 'mad' men of the 'Digression Concerning Madness', and the Aeolists are mad in this sense, deceived by their own self-conceit.

21

The learned Aeolists maintain the original cause of all things to be wind, from which principle this whole universe was at first produced, and into which it must at last be resolved; that the same breath which had kindled, and blew *up* the flame of nature, should one day blow it *out*:

Quod procul a nobis flectat Fortuna gubernans.

This is what the *adepti* understand by their *anima mundi*; that is to say, the spirit, or breath, or wind of the world; for examine the whole system by the particulars of nature, and you will find it not to be disputed. For whether you please to call the *forma informans* of man, by the name of *spiritus*, *animus*, *afflatus*, or *anima*; what are all these but several appellations for wind, which is the ruling element in every compound, and into which they all resolve upon their corruption? Farther, what is life itself, but as it is commonly called, the breath of our nostrils? . . .

In consequence of this, their next principle was, that man brings with him into the world a peculiar portion or grain of wind, which may be called a *quinta essentia*, extracted from the other four. This quintessence is of a catholic use upon all emergencies of life, is improvable into all arts and sciences, and may be wonderfully refined, as well as enlarged by certain methods in education. This, when blown up to its perfection, ought not to be covetously hoarded up, stifled, or hid under a bushel, but freely communicated to mankind. Upon these reasons, and others of equal weight, the wise Æolists affirm the gift of BELCHING to be the noblest act of a rational creature. To cultivate which art, and render it more serviceable to mankind, they made use of several methods. At certain seasons of the year, you might behold the priests amongst them, in vast numbers, with their mouths gaping wide against a storm. At other times were to be seen several hundreds linked together in a circular chain, with every man a pair of bellows applied to his neighbour's breech, by which they blew up each other to the shape and size of a tun; and for that reason, with great propriety of speech, did usually call their bodies, their vessels. When, by these and the like performances, they were grown sufficiently replete, they would immediately depart, and disembogue for the public good and plentiful share of their acquirements, into their disciples' chaps. For we must here observe, that all learning was esteemed among them to be compounded from the

93

same principle. Because, first, it is generally affirmed, or confessed that learning puffeth men up; and, secondly, they proved it by the following syllogism: Words are but wind; and learning is nothing but words; *ergo*, learning is nothing but wind. For this reason, the philosophers among them did, in their schools, deliver to their pupils, all their doctrines and opinions, by eructation, wherein they had acquired a wonderful eloquence, and of incredible variety. But the great characteristic, by which their chief sages were best distinguished, was a certain position of countenance, which gave undoubted intelligence to what degree or proportion the spirit agitated the inward mass. For, after certain gripings, the wind and vapours issuing forth, having first, by their turbulence and convulsions within, caused an earthquake in man's little world, distorted the mouth, bloated the cheeks, and gave the eyes a terrible kind of *relievo*. At which junctures all their belches were received for sacred, the sourer the better, and swallowed with infinite consolation by their meagre devotees. And to render these yet more complete, because the breath of man's life is in his nostrils, therefore the choicest, most edifying, and most enlivening belches, were very wisely conveyed through that vehicle, to give them a tincture as they passed.

A Tale of a Tub, Section VIII

The account of the Aeolists is managed, therefore, in a way that emphasises their confusion of physical causes and effects with physical ones. It turns upon a kind of pun, by means of which Swift is able to show, wittily and economically, the intellectual error of the Aeolists and so of the Dissenters. The latter laid great stress on individual reading of the Bible, and, it was said of them, tended to misunderstand it by reading it too literally. Similarly the Aeolists have taken literally certain metaphorical terms; and arguing on the basis of this first misunderstanding, they have built up their whole theology and religious practice.

'Spiritus', 'anima' and other words signifying 'the spirit' they take in their literal meaning of air, breath. And breath is wind, so a spiritual discourse among the Aeolists is a windy one, all verbiage and breath. The misapprehension is an excellent equivalent to the basic error Swift sees in Dissent (the mistaking of physical for spiritual is properly expressed in the Aeolist theology which mistakes a metaphorical expression for a literal one and so substitutes wind and bodily vapours for the breath of the spirit) and the details of an Aeolist service are logical developments of the first misapprehension.

This passage is satirically very rich because of the exactness—a kind of lunatic logic—with which the central pun is worked out and developed into both a miniature theology and a logical form of service, satirising the intellectual error and the preaching habits of Dissenting sects. One should identify and examine: the use of scriptural reference; the use of the terminology of scholastic logic, which had come to seem pedantic and foolish to Swift's generation; the methods of preaching and of *ex tempore* praying, among Dissenters, which Swift is satirising in his absurd and unpleasant physical descriptions.

The six-inch high creatures of Lilliput are perfectly conceived to show the mental and moral smallness of man, the pettiness of the concerns about which we are so pompous and self-important. For Swift, eighteenth-century party politics, with its struggles for office and for court favour, was one of the areas of human activity where such smallness and pretension could be seen. Naturally, then, the Lilliputians present to us man the political animal. Their tiny ruler, whose country measures twelve miles round, is no mere king but the mighty Emperor, 'delight and terror of the universe . . . whose head strikes against the sun'.

At court, Gulliver sees the candidates for great office competing before the Emperor, and the skill they are required to show (that of rope-dancing) is calculated by Swift to point to the kind of quality needed for political success under George I. The fact that a Lilliputian rope looks to Gulliver like a slender white thread increases our sense of the dexterous balance required for survival in the precarious world of eighteenth-century politics. Similarly the art of jumping over or crawling under a stick for the reward of what looks to Gulliver like a coloured silk thread —the ribbons of the Orders of the Garter (blue), Bath (red), and Thistle (green)—suggests both the subservience demanded by Lilliputian Emperor and Hanoverian King (this is underlined by the obsequious connotations of 'leaping' and 'creeping') and the worthlessness of the honour for which the 'great persons' compete.

Swift, of course, disapproved heartily of George I's government, led by the Whig Sir Robert Walpole. Under Walpole's leadership political life was thought by many to be more than usually corrupt, and his policies were of a kind Swift could only dislike. Walpole figures here as the supremely skilful rope-dancer Flimnap (he succeeded in staying in power for a number of years). Reldresal is thought to be Lord Carteret, a personal friend of Swift's but a political opponent in the affair of Wood's halfpence.

Many of the details of the Lilliputian political scene, and of Gulliver's relations with the Emperor and his ministers, relate to England under George I and his predecessor Queen Anne, and Swift is certainly attacking the King and Walpole in this book. But they are attacked as particular examples, in the field of political behaviour, of human self-importance and self-interest.

My gentleness and good behaviour had gained so far on the Emperor and his court, and indeed upon the army and people in general, that I began to conceive hopes of getting my liberty in a short time. I took all possible methods to cultivate this favourable disposition. The natives came by degrees to be less apprehensive of any danger from me. I would sometimes lie down, and let five or six of them dance on my hand. And at last the boys and girls would venture to come and play at hide and seek in my hair. I had now made a good progress in understanding and speaking their language. The Emperor had a mind one day to entertain me with several of the country shows, wherein they exceed all nations I have known, both for dexterity and magnificence. I was diverted with none so much as that of the rope-dancers, performed upon a slender white thread, extended about two foot, and twelve inches from the ground. Upon which I shall desire liberty, with the reader's patience, to enlarge a little.

This diversion is only practised by those persons who are candidates for great employments, and high favour, at court. They are trained in this art from their youth, and are not always of noble birth, or liberal education. When a great office is vacant either by death or disgrace (which often happens) five or six of those candidates petition the Emperor to entertain his Majesty and the court with a dance on the rope, and whoever jumps the highest without falling, succeeds in the office. Very often the chief ministers themselves are commanded to show their skill, and to convince the Emperor that they have not lost their faculty. Flimnap, the Treasurer, is allowed to cut a caper on the strait rope, at least an inch higher than any other lord in the whole empire. I have seen him do the summerset several times together upon a trencher fixed on the rope, which is no thicker than a common packthread in England. My friend Reldresal, Principal Secretary for Private Affairs,

JS—H

is, in my opinion, if I am not partial, the second after the Treasurer; the rest of the great officers are much upon a par.

These diversions are often attended with fatal accidents, whereof great numbers are on record. I my self have seen two or three candidates break a limb. But the danger is much greater when the ministers themselves are commanded to show their dexterity; for by contending to excel themselves and their fellows, they strain so far, that there is hardly one of them who hath not received a fall, and some of them two or three. I was assured that a year or two before my arrival, Flimnap would have infallibly broke his neck, if one of the King's cushions, that accidentally lay on the ground, had not weakened the force of his fall.

There is likewise another diversion, which is only shown before the Emperor and Empress, and first minister, upon particular occasions. The Emperor lays upon a table three fine silken threads of six inches long. One is blue, the other red, and the third green. These threads are proposed as prizes for those persons whom the Emperor hath a mind to distinguish by a peculiar mark of his favour. The ceremony is performed in his Majesty's great chamber of state, where the candidates are to undergo a trial of dexterity very different from the former and such as I have observed not the least resemblance of in any other country of the old or the new world. The Emperor holds a stick in his hands, both ends parallel to the horizon, while the candidates, advancing one by one, sometimes leap over the stick, sometimes creep under it backwards and forwards several times, according as the stick is advanced or depressed. Sometimes the Emperor holds one end of the stick, and the first minister the other; sometimes the minister has it entirely to himself. Whoever performs his part with most agility, and holds out the longest in leaping and creeping, is rewarded with the blue-coloured silk; the red is given to the next and the green to the third, which they all wear girt twice round the middle; and you see few great persons about this court who are not adorned with one of these girdles.

Gulliver's Travels, I, iii

Party political controversy is an example of our taking ourselves too seriously not only in Lilliput but in Brobdingnag, where the King laughs as he picks up Gulliver and asks him whether he is a Whig or a Tory. In this, as in other respects, the two voyages must be related to one another in reading. In Extract 9, the giant king (in contrast to the court Lilliputians, who are adept at complicated political manipulation) believes that good government involves only common sense, reason, justice, and lenity.

The following passage is part of Gulliver's proud (and unrealistic) description of the institutions of his country. This account of the two Houses of Parliament and the courts of justice presents them as they were meant to be when they were instituted, not as they have become; as abstract ideals rather than as bodies of actual, fallible men. What in Gulliver, the apparent writer, is naïve patriotic pride is in Swift, the true writer, devastating irony. The gap between the institutions as Gulliver describes them and the observed contemporary reality makes Gulliver's idealistic statement very effective satire; and the satire is emphasised by the giant king, who is a good man and also a sensible one with no illusions, realistically aware that any institution is only as good as its individual members. His questions to Gulliver point out exactly where things are likely, in the nature of things, to have gone wrong : how voters can be bribed, how noble families can degenerate, how institutions, however excellent, can be changed under the pressure of individual self-interest. Here again Swift naturally has in mind the institutions and customs of his own time and country; this is the political context he knows best, and moreover it is the one his readers know best, so that it, with its vivid relevance, will bring home most sharply the general lesson : that any institution depends for its continued effectiveness upon the virtue and vigilance of the people of the country.

23

Imagine with thyself courteous reader, how often I then wished for the tongue of Demosthenes or Cicero, that might have enabled me to celebrate the praise of my own dear native country in a style equal to its merits and felicity.

I began my discourse by informing his Majesty that our dominions consisted of two islands, which composed three mighty kingdoms under one sovereign, besides our plantations in America. I dwelt long upon the fertility of our soil, and the temperature of our climate. I then spoke at large upon the constitution of an English parliament, partly made up of an illustrious body called the House of Peers, persons of the noblest blood, and of the most ancient and ample patrimonies. I described that extraordinary care always taken of their education in arts and arms, to qualify them for being counsellors born to the king and kingdom, to have a share in the legislature, to be members of the highest court of judicature from whence there could be no appeal; and to be champions always ready for the defence of their prince and country by their valour, conduct and fidelity. That these were the ornament and bulwark of the kingdom, worthy followers of their most renowned ancestors, whose honour had been the reward of their virtue, from which their posterity were never once known to degenerate. To these were joined several holy persons, as part of that assembly, under the title of bishops, whose peculiar business it is to take care of religion, and of those who instruct the people therein. These were searched and sought out through the whole nation, by the prince and wisest counsellors, among such of the priesthood as were most deservedly distinguished by the sanctity of their lives, and the depth of their erudition; who were indeed the spiritual fathers of the clergy and the people.

That the other part of the parliament consisted of an assembly called the House of Commons, who were all principal gentlemen, freely picked and culled out by the people themselves, for their great abilities, and love of their country, to represent the wisdom of the whole nation. And these two bodies make up the most august assembly in Europe, to whom, in conjunction with the prince, the whole legislature is committed.

I then descended to the courts of justice, over which the judges, those venerable sages and interpreters of the law, presided, for determining the disputed rights and properties of men, as well as for the punishment of vice, and protection of innocence. I mentioned the prudent management of our treasury, the valour and achievements of our forces by sea and land. I computed the number of our people, by reckoning how many millions there might be of each religious sect, or political party among us. I did not omit even our sports and pastimes, or any other particular which I thought might redound to the honour of my country. And I finished all with a brief historical account of affairs and events in England for about an hundred years past.

This conversation was not ended under five audiences, each of several hours, and the King heard the whole with great attention, frequently taking notes of what I spoke, as well as memorandums of what questions he intended to ask me.

When I had put an end to these long discourses, his Majesty in a sixth audience, consulting his notes, proposed many doubts, queries, and objections, upon every article. He asked, what methods were used to cultivate the minds and bodies of our young nobility, and in what kind of business they commonly spent the first and teachable part of their lives. What course was taken to supply that assembly when any noble family became extinct. What qualifications were necessary in those who are to be created new lords: whether the humour of the prince, a sum of money to a court-lady, or a prime minister, or a design of strengthening a party opposite to the public interest, ever happened to be motives in those advancements. What share of knowledge these lords had in the laws of their country, and how they came by it, so as to enable them to decide the properties of their fellow-subjects in the last resort. Whether they were always so free from avarice, partialities, or want, that a bribe, or some other sinister view, could have no place among them. Whether those holy lords I spoke of were constantly promoted to that rank upon account of their knowledge in religious matters, and the sanctity of their lives; had never been compliers with the times while they were common priests, or slavish prostitute chaplains to some nobleman, whose opinions they continued servilely to follow after they were admitted into that assembly.

He then desired to know what arts were practised in electing those whom I called commoners. Whether a stranger with a strong purse might not influence the vulgar voters to choose him before their own landlords, or the most considerable gentleman in the neighbourhood. How it came to pass, that people were so violently bent upon getting into this assembly, which I allowed to be a great trouble and expense, often to the ruin of their families, without any salary or pension: because this appeared such an exalted strain of virtue and public spirit, that his Majesty seemed to doubt it might possibly not be always sincere: and he desired to know whether such zealous gentlemen could have any views of refunding themselves for the charges and trouble they were at, by sacrificing the public good to the designs of a weak and vicious prince in conjunction with a corrupted ministry. He multiplied his questions, and sifted me thoroughly upon every part of this head, proposing numberless enquiries and objections, which I think it not prudent or convenient to repeat.

Upon what I said in relation to our courts of justice, his Majesty desired to be satisfied in several points: and this I was the better able to do, having been formerly almost ruined by a long suit in chancery, which was decreed for me with costs. He asked, what time was usually spent in determining between right and wrong, and what degree of expense. Whether advocates and orators had liberty to plead in causes manifestly known to be unjust, vexatious, or oppressive. Whether party in religion or politics were observed to be of any weight in the scale of justice. Whether those pleading orators were persons educated in the general knowledge of equity, or only in provincial, national, and other local customs. Whether they or their judges had any part in penning those laws which they assumed the liberty of interpreting and glossing upon at their pleasure. Whether they had ever at different times pleaded for and against the same cause, and cited precedents to prove contrary opinions. Whether they were a rich or a poor corporation. Whether they received any pecuniary reward for pleading or delivering their opinions. And particularly whether they were ever admitted as members in the lower senate.

Gulliver's Travels, II, vi

The extracts in this volume have been chosen, and the commentaries made, with the intention of providing an introduction, a way in, to the works of a writer who is not, at first sight, altogether easy to understand. Swift's indirect way of writing, and his use of ideas and terms less familiar to us than to his contemporaries, make him often a difficult writer. But he is also a thoroughly enjoyable writer, whose attitudes and views—his sharp eye for self-deceit, complacency, or cruelty, for example—are congenial to readers in any age. It is well worth while to acquire the knowledge which will enable us to enjoy his work fully.

But extracts, however useful in providing the tools for an understanding of an author's works in their completeness, can never be a substitute for them, nor can they do full justice to them. No extract can demonstrate the sustained richness and liveliness of Swift's imagination, which constitutes so much of his charm. The consistent invention with which he gravely builds up the toy-like yet ruthless world of Lilliput, the grossness and the warmth of giant Brobdingnag, or solemn Houyhnhnm-land with its straight-faced descriptions of the rational horses sitting on their haunches to eat or to thread needles with their hooves, can only be appreciated when *Gulliver's Travels* is read as a whole. Swift's inventions often have a delightful grave absurdity which is what he calls (in one of his best poems, the humane and humorous 'Verses on the Death of Dr. Swift') his 'vein ironically grave'; and though we must be able to recognise the serious matters he wants us to think about we must also respond to the fun and the skill of the thing. Swift was known to his friends as a gay, witty, companionable and affectionate man, and the gaiety is there in much of his work, though it is true that the gaiety can be savage when he is angry enough. He thought there was a great deal wrong with the world, with society, and with individuals, but he thought too that one way to deal with foolishness or even wickedness is to laugh at it. Comedy can be a profoundly serious form, and Swift's comic satire is both serious and delightful. For how, he would have asked, can satire have any effect in the world if it is not enjoyable enough for people to read it? *Gulliver's Travels*, probably the greatest and certainly the most popular of Swift's works, shows this well. It is an unflinching exploration of the nature of man, and it is sometimes painful, for it dwells more cogently on man's disastrous pride and blindness than on his capacity for compassion and humility (though these too are quietly present), but it has continued to be read because its wit and humour and imaginative power are both attractive and convincing. It is to an appreciation of such works as these in their entirety that it is hoped this book will lead.

When once the tools for understanding have been acquired, the best scheme for further reading is to turn first to some of the shorter satires, preferably to *A Modest Proposal* and *An Argument against Abolishing Christianity*. In such short pieces it is easier to accustom one's self to Swift's 'vein ironically grave', and to see how precise a way of writing it is. The ironical presentation, through a persona, of an unacceptable point of view shows up more sharply than a straightforward denunciation could do the intellectual fallacies and moral inadequacies involved in the treatment of the Irish, or the acceptance of religion as a social convenience, and it engages our feelings more strongly. After reading these with close attention one can go on to *Gulliver's Travels* with a clearer awareness of the ironies concealed in Gulliver's simple-seeming account of his strange adventures; we perceive that the travels are so framed as to form a journey into our selves, and our possibilities for evil and for good. Swift's creative powers are at their richest in these invented lands which are yet so relevant to our own; and (provided that we keep our wits about us and remember that though Gulliver may be simple, Swift his creator is not) *Gulliver's Travels* is not a difficult book either to understand or to enjoy. *A Tale of a Tub*, however, is difficult indeed, being a complex parody of ways of writing and thinking; and this highly literary and allusive work is best read when wide reading in the less difficult works has made one sensitive to those delicate stylistic indications by which Swift lets us know where his irony is leading.

This indeed is ultimately the only way fully to know and appreciate Swift: to read as much of his work as one can, not only the major satires but more personal works, such as his charming and affectionate letters to his friends (especially those to Pope and Dr. Arbuthnot); the Journal he wrote for his dearest friend of all, Stella, when he was away in London: the prayers he said for her when she was gravely ill; the series of poems he wrote for her on her birthday. These, except for the prayers, are often ironic and indirect, though the irony here is tender and rueful, not satiric. Swift was a fine letter-writer in an age of fine letter-writers, and his poems of personal friendship are equally good. He had, indeed, a genius for friendship and its expression, notable even in the eighteenth century when such things were valued and cultivated as part of a humane and civilised life. To read widely among such pieces is to become intimately acquainted with the way Swift's mind, and his affections, work, and with the habitually ironic mode of expression which seems to have been natural to him. And it is also to discover that this most devastating of satirists is a man of deep and loyal feeling, sensitive to and careful of the feelings of those he loves and respects, though at the same time clear-sighted and astringent, never letting his friends blind themselves to the facts. We can understand better the values that made Swift a great satirist, when we read the letters or such poems as 'Verses on the Death of Dr. Swift', 'On Mrs. Biddy Floyd', 'The First of April', with its picture of family affection, and the 'Stella's Birth-Day' verses.

Reference list of Swift's writings

Only the more important works are listed separately, but all Swift's writings, including his many short political tracts, and his more ephemeral squibs in prose and verse, are available in the editions listed below. The date in brackets following each work is that of original publication. It is followed, wherever relevant, by the number of the volume of the authoritative edition of the prose, *Prose Works*, ed. Herbert Davis (14 vols.), Blackwell, Oxford, 1939, in which the work is printed.

MAJOR WORKS

A Tale of a Tub, The Battle of the Books, The Mechanical Operation of the Spirit (1704), I.
The Drapier's Letters (1724–1725), X.
Gulliver's Travels (1726), XI.

PERSONAL WRITINGS

Journal to Stella (1784; but written 1710–1713), ed. Harold Williams (2 vols.), Oxford, 1948.
Thoughts on Religion, Further Thoughts on Religion (1765), IX.

POLITICAL WRITINGS

A Discourse of the Contests and Dissensions in Athens and Rome (1701), I.
The Story of the Injured Lady (1746, written circa 1707), IX.
The Examiner (1710–1711), III.

REFERENCE LIST OF SWIFT'S WRITINGS

The Sentiments of A Church of England Man, with Respect to Religion and Government (1711), II.

The Conduct of the Allies (1711), VI.

The Importance of the Guardian Considered (1713), VIII.

The History of the Four Last Years of the Queen (1758, written 1713), VII.

The Publick Spirit of the Whigs (1714), VIII.

Some Free Thoughts Upon the Present State of Affairs (1741, written 1714), VIII.

An Enquiry into the Behaviour of the Queen's Last Ministry (1765, written circa 1717), VIII.

A Proposal for the Universal Use of Irish Manufacture (1720), IX.

A Short View of the State of Ireland (1728), XII.

Papers contributed to *The Intelligencer* (1728), XII.

A Modest Proposal (1729), XII.

Maxims Controlled in Ireland (1765, written circa 1729), XII.

WRITINGS RELATING TO RELIGION AND THE CHURCH

A Project for the Advancement of Religion and the Reformation of Manners (1709), II.

Mr. Collins's Discourse of Free Thinking Put into plain English, by way of Abstract, for the Use of the Poor (1713), IV.

An Argument against Abolishing Christianity in England (1711), II.

A Letter to a Young Gentleman, lately entered into Holy Orders (1720), IX.

Sermons (1744–1765), IX.

WRITINGS RELATING TO LITERARY MATTERS

A Proposal for Correcting the English Tongue (1712), IV.

A Letter of Advice to a Young Poet (1721), IX.

MISCELLANEOUS HUMOUROUS WORKS

The Bickerstaff Papers (1708–1709), II.

A Meditation upon a Broomstick (1710), I.

Polite Conversation (1738, but begun in 1704), IV. Also ed. Eric Partridge, Oxford University Press, London and New York.

Hints Towards an Essay on Conversation (1763, written circa 1710), IV.

Directions to Servants (1745), XIII.

Select bibliography

TEXTS

Swift's prose is best read in the 14 volume edition cited above, ed. Herbert Davis. Several of the volumes have very helpful introductory material. Other authoritative texts are

A Tale of a Tub, to which is added The Battle of the Books and The Mechanical Operation of the Spirit, ed. A. C. Guthkelch and D. Nichol Smith, Clarendon Press, Oxford, 1729, second edition 1958. This is annotated in great detail.
The Poems of Jonathan Swift, ed. Harold Williams (3 vols.), Clarendon Press, Oxford, 1937, second edition 1958.
The Correspondence of Jonathan Swift, ed. Harold Williams (5 vols.), Oxford University Press, London, 1963.

Useful working collections are

Gulliver's Travels and Other Writings, ed. Louis A. Landa, Riverside Press, Cambridge, Mass., 1960.
Gulliver's Travels and Selected Writings in Prose and Verse, ed. John Hayward, London and New York, 1934.
Jonathan Swift, A Selection of his Works, ed. Philip Pinkus, Macmillan, Toronto, London, and New York, 1965.
Satires and Personal Writings, ed. W. A. Eddy, Oxford University Press, London and New York, 1932.
Swift on his Age, Selected Prose and Verse, ed. Colin J. Horne, Harrap, London, 1953.
Collected Poems, ed. Joseph Horrell (2 vols.), Muses Library, London, 1958.

SELECT BIBLIOGRAPHY

BIOGRAPHY

EHRENPREIS, IRVIN, *Swift, The Man, His Works, and the Age.* Vol. I, *Mr. Swift and His Contemporaries*, Methuen, London, and Harvard University Press, Cambridge, Mass., 1962. The most dependable biography; only one volume so far published.

EHRENPREIS, IRVIN, *The Personality of Jonathan Swift*, Methuen, London, Harvard University Press, Cambridge, Mass., 1958. A collection of biographical and critical essays.

JACKSON, R. WYSE, *Jonathan Swift, Dean and Pastor*, S.P.C.K., London, 1939. Concentrates on Swift's life and work as clergyman.

LANDA, LOUIS A., *Swift and the Church of Ireland*, Oxford, 1954. An excellent but specialised study of Swift's work for and relation to the Church of Ireland.

CRITICISM

General

BEAUMONT, C. A., *Swift's Classical Rhetoric*, University of Georgia Monographs No. 8, Athens, Georgia, 1961. Closely examines several shorter satires; demonstrates Swift's skilful use of formal classical rhetoric.

BULLITT, JOHN M., *Jonathan Swift and the Anatomy of Satire*, Harvard University Press, Cambridge, Mass., Oxford University Press, London, 1953. Good general treatment of satiric methods.

DAVIS, HERBERT, *The Satire of Jonathan Swift*, Macmillan, New York, 1947. Essays on the literary, political, and moral satire.

EWALD, W. B., *The Masks of Jonathan Swift*, Harvard University Press, Cambridge, Mass., Blackwell, Oxford, 1954. Detailed examination of the satiric personae.

FERGUSON, OLIVER W., *Jonathan Swift and Ireland*, University of Illinois Press, Urbana, Illinois, 1962. A useful setting of the Irish satires into their historical background.

PRICE, MARTIN, *Swift's Rhetorical Art*, Yale University Press, New Haven, 1953. A valuable and readable general study.

QUINTANA, R., *The Mind and Art of Jonathan Swift*, Oxford University Press, London and New York, 1936; Methuen, London, 1953, A very inclusive treatment; life as well as works.

Swift, An Introduction, Oxford University Press, London, 1955. Very useful introductory short study; essays on various aspects of Swift's work, covering his entire career.

ROSENHEIM, EDWARD R., *Swift and the Satirist's Art*, University of Chicago Press, 1965.

TUVESON, ERNEST, ed., *Swift: A Collection of Critical Essays*, Twentieth Century Views Series, Prentice-Hall, Eaglewood Cliffs, New

Jersey, 1964. Some of the most important essays previously published in journals.

VOIGT, MILTON, *Swift and the Twentieth Century*, Wayne University Press, Detroit, 1964. A survey of major modern developments in criticism, biography, and textual studies.

WILLIAMS, KATHLEEN, *Jonathan Swift and the Age of Compromise*, University of Kansas Press, Lawrence, Kansas, 1958, Constable, London, 1959.

The Battle of the Books

JONES, RICHARD FOSTER, *Ancients and Moderns, a Study of the Background of the Battle of the Books*, Washington University Studies, New series, Lang. and Lit. no. 6, St. Louis, Missouri, 1936. Valuable study of the Ancients and Moderns controversy.

A Tale of a Tub

HARTH, PHILLIP, *Swift and Anglican Rationalism. The Religious Background of A Tale of a Tub*, University of Chicago Press, 1961. Relates *Tale* to seventeenth-century religious controversy.

PAULSON, RONALD, *Theme and Structure in Swift's Tale of a Tub*, Yale University Press, New Haven, Conn., 1960. A fine discussion of the complex methods of the *Tale* as embodying Swift's criticism of man.

STARKMAN, MIRIAM K., *Swift's Satire on Learning in A Tale of a Tub*, Princeton University Press, 1950. Examines the sources Swift drew upon for the Digressions.

Gulliver's Travels

This is extensively treated in all the general works. Specialised studies are

CASE, ARTHUR E., *Four Essays on Gulliver's Travels*, Princeton University Press, 1945. Partly critical; also discusses the establishing of the correct text.

EDDY, WILLIAM A., *Gulliver's Travels, a Critical Study*, Princeton University Press, 1923. Includes discussion of sources and influences.

NICOLSON, MARJORIE, and MOHLER, NORA M., 'The Scientific Background of Swift's Voyage to Laputa', *Annals of Science*, 2, 1937; reprinted in Nicolson, M., *Science and Imagination*, Cornell University Press, Ithaca, New York, Oxford University Press, London, 1956. Examines Swift's handling of his sources in the Proceedings of the Royal Academy.

WILLIAMS, HAROLD, *The Text of Gulliver's Travels*, Cambridge University Press, 1952. Wholly bibliographical study.